MW01181916

The Bible
in a
Nutshell

Introduction to Sixty-six of the Greatest Books Ever Written

By Lou Nicholes

PRESS

Copyright © 2003 by Lou Nicholes

The Bible in a Nutshell
by Lou Nicholes

Printed in the United States of America

ISBN 1-594671-06-0

Unless otherwise indicated, Scripture quotations are from the King James Version of the Bible. This book is a compilation of material from many and varied resources over the past forty years. It comes from notes taken during classroom instruction at Bible school, lectures in various seminars, and sermon preparation notes over the years. It is impossible for me to name all the people, books, and sources from which this was gathered. I just appreciate this wealth of information that God has allowed me to glean over the years and appreciate all the people who have contributed to this effort.

Xulon Press
www.XulonPress.com

Xulon Press books are available in bookstores everywhere,
and on the Web at www.XulonPress.com.

Dedicated to

Thelma, my wonderful wife and helpmate

"A virtuous woman is a crown to her husband."
(Proverbs 12:4)

AN INTRODUCTION TO THE BIBLE

T he Bible is by far the most popular book in the world. Portions of it have been translated in over two thousand languages, and it has been copied and circulated more extensively than any other literature. Many have sought to ban and destroy the Bible, but their efforts have been futile. In spite of persecution, perversion, criticism, abuse, and time, the Bible has survived and is unique in its preservation.

The Bible is a unique book. It is a progressive revelation that harmoniously traces redemption from Genesis to Revelation as it centers on the person and work of Jesus Christ. The Bible was produced over a time span of about fifteen hundred years by more than forty authors who came from many diverse backgrounds. These include kings, prophets, musicians, poets, teachers, farmers, carpenters, fisherman, a tax collector, a doctor, and a tent maker. Some of these were highly educated while others were unschooled. Its chapters were written in cities and in the wilderness, in palaces and in prison, in times of war and in times of peace, and in many other circumstances of life.

The Bible contains history, law, hymns, poetry, biographies, parables, letters, philosophy, and sermons. It has many literary styles and diverse themes, and yet it never contradicts itself. Its proclamations are unique and the subject matter covers the whole range from heaven to hell, from the divine to the demonic, and from eternity past to eternity future. It describes the fall of man from his original perfect state and his sinful condition. Then it explains over and over the message of salvation by faith and not by works. As no other book it has molded and dominated morality, literature, philosophy, law, and politics in the world. It has not only changed history, but it has also changed millions of lives through its witness of the redemptive work of Christ and has brought joy, hope, and purpose for all who have appropriated it.

The Bible was divinely designed to change lives in a radical way and is relevant to all times and cultures. As Hebrews 4:12 states, "For the word of God is quick, and powerful, and sharper than any twoedged sword, piercing even to the dividing asunder of soul and spirit, and of the joints and marrow, and is a discerner of the thoughts and intents of the heart." Without a broad overview, we would miss the harmony, teaching, and significance of the Bible. It is with this in mind that this book, *The Bible in a Nutshell,* was written. We trust that the introduction, overview, and outline of each of the sixty-six books will help you gain a new perspective and appreciation for the Bible.

The Bible points out to us in several locations the one and only way we can be sure of going to heaven when we die. John 14:6 states in Jesus words, "I am the way, the truth, and the life: no man cometh unto the Father, but by me." One place this is outlined for us in a very simple way is in the book of Romans. (1) All have sinned (Rom 3:23). (2) The wages of sin is death (Rom. 6:23). (3) God loved us so much that He sent his Son to die for us (Rom. 5:8). (4) All we need to do is believe in Him with our heart and confess to Him with our mouth (Rom. 10:9-10). (5) If we call on His name we shall be saved (Rom. 10:13). This is all provided by the "death, burial and resurrection of Jesus Christ" (I Cor. 15:3-4). If you haven't taken this step of faith you can do it now and your eternal destiny will be in heaven forever.

CONTENTS

Old Testament

New Testament

	Book	**Title**

INTRODUCTION TO GENESIS
The Book of Beginnings

- Genesis means "origin" or "beginnings." It is a book about the beginning of many things: the world, man, sin, civilization, the nations, and Israel.

- "The Book of Beginnings" sets the stage for the entire Bible. It reveals the person and work of God, the value and dignity of human beings, the tragedy and consequences of sin, and the promise and assurance of salvation.

- Genesis covers the period of time from the creation of the world to the death of Joseph.

- Moses, the great Hebrew lawgiver who led the Jews out of Egypt and into Canaan, wrote the book under the inspiration of the Holy Spirit in about 1500 B.C.

- It covers a span of about three hundred years and describes events occurring as far east as Ur of the Chaldees and as far west as Egypt, but for the most part in Palestine.

- Three great questions of life are answered in Genesis:

  1. Where did I come from? (1:1)
  2. Why am I here? (15:6)
  3. Where am I going? (25:8)

- Genesis provides a dramatic account of the origin of the universe, the origin of mankind, the intrusion of sin into the world and the devastating effects of its curse on the human race, and the beginnings of God's plan to bless the nations through His seed.

- The personal accounts of great men, women, and families of God are recorded in Genesis. The lives of Adam and Eve, Abraham and Sarah, Noah, Isaac, Jacob, Esau, and Joseph are all told about in detail.

- Genesis supplies the historical background for God's covenant with His people. This can then be traced through the five books of the law known as the Pentateuch.

- Genesis can be outlined at follows:

1. Creation of the world (chapters 1–2).
2. Sin enters the world (chapters 3–4).
3. Noah and the flood (chapters 5–9).
4. Beginning of nations and languages (chapters 10–11).
5. Abraham's family and God's people in the land (chapters 12–38).
6. Joseph and God's people going to Egypt (chapters 39–50).

INTRODUCTION TO EXODUS
The Book of Redemption

• Historically, Exodus records the events of Israel's deliverance from Egypt after four hundred years of oppression and slavery under Pharaoh the king.

• God rescued Israel through its leader, Moses, and through mighty miracles.

• The three parts in the drama of redemption are: enslavement, separation, and sanctification.

• There is no reason to doubt that the Holy Spirit inspired Moses to write this book. Jesus declared that Moses was the author (Mark 12:26).

• Several basic types can be found in this book:

   1. Egypt is a type of the world.
   2. Pharaoh is a type of Satan.
   3. Israel is a type of the church.
   4. Moses is a type of Christ.
   5. Manna is a type of Christ, the bread of life.
   6. Amalek is a type of the flesh.
   7. The Passover is a type of the death of Christ.

• The journey through the wilderness with its trials and testings and with God's provision to meet every need represents the experience of our lives.

• Exodus relates more miracles than any other book in the Old Testament and is noted for containing the Ten Commandments.

- Key people in the book are Moses, Miriam, Pharaoh, Pharaoh's daughter, Jethro, Aaron, Joshua, and Bezaleel.

- Key places are Goshen, the Nile River, Midian, the Red Sea, and Mount Sinai.

- Doctrinally it deals with redemption, and its contents can be outlined in five divisions:

  1. The need for redemption: Pictures a people enslaved (chapters 1–6).
  2. The power of the redeemer: Displayed in the plagues (chapters 7–11).
  3. The character of redemption: Purchased by blood (chapters 12–18).
  4. The duty of the redeemed: Obedience to the Lord (chapters 19–24).
  5. Provisions for failures of the redeemed (chapters 25–40).

INTRODUCTION TO LEVITICUS
Provisions for Holy Living

* After Israel's dramatic exit from Egypt, the nation was camped at the foot of Mount Sinai for two years to listen to God (Exodus 19 to Numbers 10). It was a time of resting, teaching, and meeting with Him face to face.

* Worship and service are the central themes of the book of Leviticus.

* Most Bible scholars believe that Moses wrote the first five books of the Bible, including Leviticus.

* Leviticus received its name from the word "Levites," who were the people God chose to be priests and workers in the Tabernacle.

* The overwhelming message of Leviticus is the holiness of God: "Ye shall be holy: for I the Lord your God am holy" (19:2).

* The book of Leviticus has laws about offerings, priests, food, health, daily life, feasts, rewards, and punishments.

* The final emphasis in Leviticus is celebration. There were special, regular, and corporate occasions for remembering what God had done, giving thanks to Him, and rededicating lives to His service

* As you read Leviticus, rededicate yourself to holiness, worshiping God in private and in group worship.

- The following is a suggested outline of the book:

  1. Laws about offerings. These offerings included animals, grain, and other items that would be placed on the altar. Different sacrifices were required for different purposes (chapters 1–7).
  2. Laws about the priests. These were strict laws about the duties and behavior of the priests (chapters 8–10).
  3. Laws about food, health, and daily life. Many of these laws concerned standards of health and the cleanliness of the camp (chapters 11–22).
  4. Laws about feasts. God gave careful directions about how the people should celebrate holy days (chapters 23–25).
  5. Laws concerning rewards and punishments. Directions were given for how to make a promise, how to give to God, and what to expect when God was not obeyed (chapters 26–27).

INTRODUCTION TO NUMBERS
Wilderness Wanderings

- Numbers is about the wilderness wanderings of the people of Israel from Mount Sinai to the border of Canaan, the Promised Land.

- The book starts out at Mount Sinai and ends on the plains of Moab. Its narrative picks up where Exodus left off and connects with Deuteronomy, which starts on the east side of the Jordan in the wilderness.

- Many contrasting themes are woven throughout Numbers: God's faithfulness and human failures, God's guidance and human stubbornness, God's purpose and human disobedience, God's provision and human complaints, and God's holiness and human sinfulness.

- God's twofold plan was to *reveal His faithfulness* through provision and deliverance and to relate His law, which prepared Israel to maintain a covenant relationship with the Lord, and to *fulfill the task* of being God's people in the midst of an ungodly world.

- As the "children of Israel" journeyed from the foot of Mount Sinai to the land of Canaan, they grumbled, whined, and complained at every turn. First they complained about the food. Next, about Moses' authority. God punished some but spared the nation because of Moses' prayers.

- Numbers also gives a clear example of God's patience. Again and again He withholds judgment and preserves the nation. But His patience must not be taken for granted, for His time of judgment will come.

- When the nation arrived at Kadesh, twelve spies (one for each tribe) were sent into Canaan to assess its strength. Ten returned with fearful stories of giants. Only Caleb and Joshua encouraged them to "go up at once, and possess it" (13:30).

- Because of their unbelief, God declared that the present generation would not live to see the Promised Land. Instead, they wandered in the wilderness for forty years with a continuous pattern of grumbling, defiance, discipline, and death.

- Numbers is probably the last book most people would choose for devotional reading. However, for any reader willing to put forth some effort in study, Numbers is far from dull.

- The events in this book took about forty years and can be outlined as follows:

  1. The preparation for the journey (chapters 1–10).
  2. The wilderness wanderings (chapters 11–20).
  3. The journey to Canaan (chapters 21–36).

INTRODUCTION TO DEUTERONOMY
Moses' Final Instructions

• Deuteronomy is the fifth of the first five books of the Bible called the "Books of the Law"or the Pentateuch. Deuteronomy means "Second Law," which simply indicates that the Ten Commandments are repeated (Exodus 20). This was written to remind the people of what God did for them. Much of Deuteronomy is repetition and explanation of the three preceding books.

• The book of Deuteronomy (except the final summary by Joshua) was written by Moses just prior to his death and before Israel entered into the Promised Land. Israel was now perched at the entrance to the Promised Land (1:5) as they received Moses' final instructions.

• Keep in mind that these words came from a man who was 120 years old. He had led three million Jews in the wilderness for forty years.

• The key words are "remember" (fourteen times), "hear" (over thirty times), and "do" (about one hundred).

• In this book, Moses summed up the essential contents of all the commandments, statutes, and obligations that God had commanded. He exhorted the people to be obedient and gave them promises of blessings if they should obey and threats of punishment if they should disobey.

• When Moses was giving directions from the Lord, he told the people that Canaan was "a land whose stones are iron, and out of whose hills thou mayest dig brass [copper]" (8:9). Recent discoveries have proven that there is copper in the hills of which Moses spoke. In fact, these copper mines were probably in use during the days of Solomon.

- Moses spent forty years in Pharaoh's palace, forty years in Midian, and forty years leading Israel in the wilderness, which involved transplanting three million people from one land to another.

- A brief outline of Deuteronomy is as follows:

  1. A retrospect of Israel's wanderings (chapters 1–4). Moses' first speech to the people. *Looking back:* He reminded the people of God's faithfulness in their journey from Egypt.
  2. A rehearsal of Israel's law (chapters 5–26). Moses' second speech to the people. *Looking up:* He reviewed God's laws and warned the people not to anger God by disobeying Him.
  3. A renewal of Israel's covenant (chapters 27–34). Moses' third speech to the people. *Looking out:* He reviewed the agreement between God and the people and assured them of God's continual protection.

INTRODUCTION TO JOSHUA
Conquest of the Promised Land

- Joshua is a book of biblical history that tells of the conquest and settlement of the Hebrew nation in Palestine after her forty years of wilderness wandering.

- Most of the book of Joshua is thought to have been written by Joshua himself. However, Joshua 24 was written after his death, so it must have been written by someone else; some think it was Eleazar the priest.

- The events of Joshua begin where those of Deuteronomy conclude.

- Joshua, the son of Nun of the tribe of Ephraim, was born while Israel was in her four hundred years of Egyptian slavery. He was the one God chose to take over after Moses died.

- It is believed that Joshua was forty years of age at the time of the Exodus and was nearly eighty-five years old when he took Moses' place as head of the nation.

- Throughout the wilderness journey, Joshua stood at the side of Moses in the task of leading three million people on their march to Canaan.

- Joshua, along with eleven others, was chosen by Moses to spy out the land of Canaan. As a result, Joshua and Caleb were the only two who had the faith to believe that Israel could conquer the land with God's help.

- The land of Canaan, originally promised to Abraham's

seed, extended from the river of Egypt to the great river Euphrates (Genesis 15:18). God described the land as one of hills and valleys, blessed with rain, that He cared for Himself throughout all the seasons (Deuteronomy 11:11–12).

- The enemy that Israel faced in this land was not one unified nation but was occupied by the Hittites, Jebusites, Amorites, etc., who had been repeatedly warned by God over hundreds of years (Genesis 15:16–21) to repent of their immoral practices and filthy ways.

- The book can be outlined as follows:

  1. Conquering the land (chapters 1–12). Joshua prepared for battle (1), spies were sent out (2), they crossed the Jordan (3–5), walls came down (6), they were defeated at Ai (7–8), and Joshua was tricked into defending Gibeon (9–12).
  2. Dividing the land (chapters 13–22). Divided between the twelve tribes of Israel. Levi was chosen to serve as priests and Joseph was represented by his sons Ephraim and Manasseh.
  3. Joshua's farewell and death (chapters 23–24).

INTRODUCTION TO JUDGES
Apostasy and Failure of the Israelites

- After the death of Joshua, Israel had judges instead of kings to rule.

- No clear statement or indication of authorship occurs in the book, but many Bible scholars think Samuel was the author.

- Judges is filled with sensational stories, as exciting as any of today's headlines. It includes gruesome murders, sexual exploits, and superhuman feats of strength.

- It was a period of terrible apostasy and immorality.

- The period of the Judges is thought to have covered approximately three hundred years, but it could have been longer.

- This book records seven apostasies, seven servitudes to seven heathen nations, and seven deliverances.

- Twelve different judges are named in this book (some add Abimelech).

- The chief judges were Deborah, Gideon, Samson, and Samuel.

- Five of the judges about whom we know very little were Tola, Jair, Ibzan, Elon, and Abdon.

- The judges were chosen by God to deliver the Israelites and then rule with justice.

- Judges echoes with rebellion, retribution, repentance, and restoration. Then the same cycle repeats itself all over again, some six or seven times.

- Each judge was divinely appointed and called out for a particular crisis.

- Archaeology shows that the superpowers of Babylonia, Assyria, and Egypt were relatively weak during the days of the judges.

- In general, the book of Judges is one of failures on the part of God's people to trust His word and claim His power.

- Warren Wiersbe gives the following suggested outline:

  1. Apathy: Israel's wars (chapters 1–2).
  2. Apostasy: Israel's woes (chapters 3–16).
  3. Anarchy: Israel's ways (chapters 17–21).

INTRODUCTION TO RUTH
The Virtuous Woman

• The author is unknown.

• This book is thought to have been written during the reign of David or Solomon and covers the period of the judges.

• This heartwarming story of devotion and faithfulness records the life of Ruth, a Moabite widow who left her homeland to live with her widowed Jewish mother-in-law in Bethlehem during a time of famine in Israel.

• Ruth, the heroine of this book, had several strikes against her. In this culture, people honored women with children; she had none. Women were dependent on their husbands; she was a widow. Communities were close-knit; she was a foreigner.

• The theme of redemption permeates this book. Ruth was transformed from poverty to wealth, widow to wife, barren to fertile, and foreigner to Israelite.

• Ruth, who had married one of the sons who died, decided to return to Bethlehem of Israel with her mother-in-law, Naomi.

• For Ruth, this meant leaving the god of the Moabites (Chemosh) whose worship involved wild celebrations and even the rite of human sacrifice.

• Boaz, a kinsman-redeemer who gave Ruth and Naomi a new life, is a key figure in the book.

- The three men of the family died during the ten years spent in Moab.

- An outline of the book:

  1. The tragedies of Moab (1:1–18).
  2. The return to Bethlehem (1:19–22).
  3. The fields of Boaz (2:1–23).
  4. The marriage proposal (3:1–18).
  5. The kinsman-redeemer (4:1–12).
  6. The marriage of Ruth and Boaz (4:13–17).
  7. The genealogy of David (4:18–22).

INTRODUCTION TO I SAMUEL
From Theocracy to Monarchy

- I Samuel records the life of Samuel, who was Israel's last judge. It describes Israel's transition period from a theocracy (led by God) to a monarchy (led by a king). It covers the reign and decline of Saul, the first king, and the choice and preparation of David.

- Eli began the race of life with a close relationship with God. In chapters 1–3, he demonstrated a clear understanding of God's purposes and call as Israel's high priest. However, his life ended in tragedy as his undisciplined and sacrilegious sons desecrated the temple.

- Samuel, who was dedicated to the service of God by his mother, Hannah, became one of Israel's greatest prophets. However, like Eli's family, Samuel's sons turned away from God as they took bribes and perverted justice.

- Saul started out as a handsome (9:2) and humble man (9:21; 10:22) who was God's choice as the first king of Israel (10:24). Later he disobeyed God and became a very jealous old man who was obsessed with killing David. Finally, his life ended in suicide.

- David was another great beginner who ministered to Saul (chapter 6) and became a great warrior. He waited patiently for God to deal with Saul after he was anointed to be Israel's next king. However, when his name is mentioned today, everyone remembers his sin with Bathsheba and how he had her husband killed.

- During this period of time, Israel's neighbors played a significant role in the outworking of God's providence:

  1. The Philistines controlled southwest Palestine and oppressed Israel for forty years.
  2. The Ammonites settled east of the Jordan River, and partly because of their threat, Israel came to Samuel and asked for a king.
  3. The Edomites controlled the territory south of the Dead Sea and were made up of the descendants of Esau, who were mostly farmers.
  4. The Moabites inhabited territory north of Edom, where David sought safety for his parents when he ran from Saul.
  5. The Canaanites, descendants from Noah's son Ham, occupied territory inside the Promised Land, and constituted a threat to Israel's spiritual well-being.
  6. The Amorites migrated from Upper Mesopotamia and mingled with the Canaanites.

- I Samuel can be divided as follows:

  1. Samuel—Israel's last judge (chapters 1–8).
  2. Saul—Israel's first king (chapters 9–13).

INTRODUCTION TO II SAMUEL
David's Triumphs and Trials

- This book traces the history of Israel from the death of Saul to the end of David's reign. We get a special glimpse of God's hand in human events. David rose to power because God selected him. We see how David's heroic exploits were possible because God was with him. We see David's disappointments show God's justice and mercy.

- It is not known for sure who wrote the book of II Samuel, but it tells David's story and is named after the prophet who anointed David and guided him in living for God.

- The book records David's crowning as king over Judah in Hebron, and then king over all of Israel in Jerusalem (1–5). Chapter 6 tells how he brought the ark of the covenant back to the tabernacle. From here through chapter 10, it tells how he sustained victory after victory on the battlefield. However, he was not always victorious.

- The record of lust, adultery, and murder is not easy reading as we see how David stumbled and fell into sin with Bathsheba (11–12). He also had serious family problems as his son Amnon raped his sister Tamar. When David found out about this, he was very angry, but he did not punish Amnon. When his son Absalom learned about the rape, he began to hate his brother and ended up murdering Amnon (13).

- This was not the end of David's family problems as Absalom caused the entire nation to rebel against David and crowned himself king. Eventually he was defeated and died (14–18). After this, the kingdom was in disarray, but David was able to take charge once again and successfully ruled until he turned it over to his son Solomon forty years later.

- The story of this fallen hero does not end in tragedy. Through repentance, his fellowship and peace with God were restored, but he had to suffer the consequences of the sins he committed. The consequences stayed with him the rest of his life as a reminder of his sinful deeds and his need for God.

- In spite of David's terrible sin, he was a king who governed God's people by God's principles and one whom God blessed. As we read this book, we see his characteristics of faithfulness, patience, courage, generosity, honesty, modesty, and penitence. We can learn valuable lessons from his sins and his repentance.

- John Phillips in his book titled *Exploring the Scriptures* outlines II Samuel as follows:

  1. The patient years (chapters 1–4).
  2. The prosperous years (chapters 5–12).
  3. The perilous years (chapters 13–24).

INTRODUCTION TO I KINGS
The Kingdom Divided

• I and II Kings were appropriately named as they are a record of the reigns of all the kings of Judah and Israel except Saul. They begin with David's last days and the events of placing Solomon on the throne through the fall of the Jewish monarchy and the destruction of Jerusalem in 586 B.C. These two books were originally one volume, but later became two.

• The setting for this book is that the chosen people had been conquered and were in exile; Babylon was in control of the Promised Land; Jerusalem lay in ruins; the temple had been destroyed; and Jehoiachin, David's descendant, was a captive. In this time of disruption, the exiles wondered what had happened to God's promises to His people.

• The human authorship of I and II Kings is not known. It could have been Ezra, a priest who had strong feelings for the history of the people, or it could have been the prophet Ezekiel or the prophet Jeremiah. The Jewish Talmud states that Jeremiah wrote Kings.

• More important is the fact that these books were not only written to record history, but also to teach the lessons of history. They reveal:

1. The pitiful shortcomings of man. God repeatedly gave these rulers an opportunity to forsake sin and turn to Him, but again and again they resisted.
2. The character of God. Dr. Charles Woodbridge once said, "His grace is amazing, his patience is

enduring, His compassion is infinite, but His justice is inflexible."

3. The importance of the prophets of God. False prophets were numerous, but great men of God such as Elijah, Elisha, Isaiah, Jeremiah, and Jonah crossed the pages of Jewish history with dignity and majesty.

4. A true philosophy of history. These words were penned not only to record facts of historical significance, but also to reveal and preserve spiritual lessons that have timeless value.

• The story of Solomon, the wisest man who ever lived, is found in this book, along with accounts of other kings of this time. They provide us with both positive examples to follow and mistakes to avoid. It is here that we learn about the tragic division of Israel into the northern kingdom (Israel) and the southern kingdom (Judah). This division sets the stage for the rest of biblical history.

• An outline of I Kings:

1. United kingdom: Kingdom in tranquility (chapters 1–11).

2. Divided kingdom: Kingdom in turmoil (chapters 12–22).

INTRODUCTION TO II KINGS
Spiritual Climate Determines Economic Conditions

• II Kings continues with the happenings and destinies of the two kingdoms (Israel and Judah) that began in I Kings. Israel was captured and dispersed by the Assyrians, while Judah was placed in exile in Babylonia. The kingdoms were divided in I Kings but they were dissolved in II Kings.

• It is not certain who wrote this book, but according to ancient Jewish tradition, Jeremiah did. Originally it was written to preserve the history of Israel and Judah for the Jews living in exile in Babylon. It appears that the author wanted his readers to learn the lessons of history, reminding them of the consequences of unfaithfulness to God.

• The books of Kings were originally one book but were split into two in the third century by those who translated the Old Testament into Greek. II Kings covers over two hundred years from the ministry of Elisha under Ahaziah, king of Israel, and Jehoram, king of Judah, to the fall of the kingdom of Judah.

• In this book we read of evil rulers, rampant idolatry, and a complacent population that was going in a downward spiral. Despite the pressure to conform, to turn from the Lord, and to serve only self, a minority of people moved the opposite direction, toward God. The Bethel prophets and others, as well as two righteous kings, spoke God's word and stood for Him.

• The author systematically traced the reigning monarchs of both Israel and Judah. Judah lasted 136 years longer than Israel did. Eight of Judah's twenty kings had godly ways while Israel had nineteen consecutive evil kings, and they never broke away from Jeroboam's idolatrous calf worship.

- During these years, God sent His prophets Elijah, Elisha, Amos, and Hosea into the northern kingdom, and Obadiah, Joel, Isaiah, Micah, Nahum, Zephaniah, Jeremiah, and Habakkuk into the southern kingdom. We see how the spiritual climate of the nation determined both its political and economic conditions.

- An outline for the book:

  1. Chapters 1–17 record the history of Israel's corruption as it was led by bad kings from Ahaziah to Hosea. All but one of its nine dynasties were created by murdering the previous king. This dark period was interrupted only by Elijah and Elisha.
  2. Chapters 18–25 trace the history of Judah, and because of exemplary faith and reforms, God not only spared Jerusalem from Assyria but also brought them a measure of prosperity. However, Hezekiah's son, Manasseh, was so idolatrous that his long reign led to the downfall of Judah. Even Josiah's latter reforms could not stem the tide of evil, and the four kings who follow him were very wicked. Judah finally collapsed, resulting in the Babylonian exile.

INTRODUCTION TO I CHRONICLES
Rediscovering Our Foundation

• The genealogies of I Chronicles present an overview of Israel's history. The first nine chapters are filled with genealogies that trace the lineages of people from Adam to the exile in Babylon. Saul's death is recorded in chapter 10. Chapter 11 begins the history of David's reign.

• I Chronicles was written after the Jews returned to Jerusalem around 538 B.C. from exile in Babylon. This was the result of a decree of Cyrus, king of Persia, who authorized the return.

• This book was written from a priestly point of view and emphasizes the religious history of Judah and Israel. The northern kingdom is virtually ignored, David's triumphs—not his sins—are recalled, and the temple is given great prominence as the vital center for worship.

• Though not specifically named in the book, Ezra has been assumed to be the author.

• The purpose of the book is to trace the Davidic line and to teach that genuine worship needs to be the center of both individual and national life.

• The author evidently compiled the Chronicles to emphasize the importance of social and religious purity, and the place of the law, the temple, and the priesthood. It is apparent that he purposed not only to write history, but also to teach doctrinal and moral truth.

• It seems that the writer was not writing a complete

history of Israel but presumed his readers' knowledge of the books of Samuel and Kings. If Chronicles were read by itself, it would give an unbalanced picture of Israelite history.

• I Chronicles is also an invaluable supplement to II Samuel and a strong reminder for tracing our roots and rediscovering our foundation. It is good to trace our own godly heritage, thank God for our spiritual forefathers, and recommit ourselves to passing on God's truth to the next generation.

• David loved the Lord and wanted to build a temple to replace the tabernacle, but God denied his request. David's greatest contribution to the temple was not the construction but the preparation.

• A basic outline for I Chronicles is:

1. Genealogy: Ancestry (chapters 1–9).
2. History: Activity (chapters 10–29).

INTRODUCTION TO II CHRONICLES
Obedience and Apostasy

- I and II Chronicles were once together as one book.

- It is a history book starting with Adam (I Chronicles 1:1) and ending with Cyrus of Persia (II Chronicles 36:23) in 538 B.C.

- The word "Chronicles" refers to record books or diaries.

- The author of I and II Chronicles is not mentioned, but tradition suggests that it was Ezra.

- II Chronicles records the history of the reign of King Solomon and all of the kings of Judah from Rehoboam through Zedekiah. It focuses only on the kings of Judah and excludes those of Israel.

- More than half of I and II Chronicles has parallels in I and II Samuel and I and II Kings.

- Nearly all biblical scholars agree that I and II Chronicles could not have been written later than the end of the fifth century B.C., perhaps around 400. One reason for this is that the last person mentioned in I and II Chronicles is Anani of the eighth generation from Jehoiachin (I Chronicles 3:24). Jehoiachin was taken captive by the Babylonians in 598 B.C. If twenty-five years are allotted for each generation, Anani would have been born between 425 and 400 B.C. This would place the book between 598 and 400 B.C.

- II Chronicles repeats many stories from the books of Kings. It focuses on kings in David's family, Solomon, and the kings of Judah. You need to read the books of Kings for stories of the kings of Israel.

- Solomon enjoyed a peaceful and prosperous reign of forty years. He achieved much in business and government, but most important, he was the man God used to build the temple.

- Throughout the reigns of twenty kings, the nation of Judah wavered between obedience to God and apostasy. There were a few good kings and many evil ones. Although idolatry and injustice were common, some kings turned to God and led the people in revival. This included the destruction of idols, obedience to the law, and restoration of the priesthood.

- This book contains two major thoughts:

  1. Solomon, David's son, became the richest and wisest king on earth. He made the nation strong and built a beautiful temple in Jerusalem (chapters 1–9).
  2. The people of Israel were divided into two nations: Israel and Judah. These chapters tell about the kings of Judah (chapters 10–36).

INTRODUCTION TO EZRA
The Building of the Temple

- The books of Ezra, Esther, and Nehemiah cover the historical period of Israel's captivity in Babylon and the period immediately following their return to Jerusalem.

- In the Hebrew Bible, the books of Ezra and Nehemiah are one book. Ezra is concerned with the building of the temple. Nehemiah is concerned with the building of the city and the walls of Jerusalem.

- The book of Ezra begins right where II Chronicles leaves off (II Chronicles 36:22 and Ezra 1:1). This is one reason why it is felt that Ezra wrote both books. The book divides very naturally in line with the ministries of two men: Zerubbabel, in chapters 1 through 6; and Ezra, in chapters 7 through 10. Both of these men led the captives of Babylon back to Jerusalem.

- Sandwiched between these two accounts is a gap of nearly six decades during which Esther lived and ruled as queen in Persia.

- The book of Ezra is a simple and straightforward account of one of the most important events in Jewish history. It was written by Ezra, a priest, a scribe, and a great leader, and covers a period of over eighty years. It centers around God and His promise that the Jews would return to their land after seventy years of captivity in Babylon (Jeremiah 25:11).

1. Chapter 1 – Cyrus, king of Persia, conquered Babylon

and granted permission to the Jews to return to their homeland.

2. Chapter 2 – The first caravan of approximately fifty thousand returned to Jerusalem under the leadership of Zerubbabel.

3. Chapter 3 – After arriving, they began to build the altar and the temple foundation.

4. Chapter 4 – Local opposition arose, and accusations and rumors temporarily halted the project.

5. Chapter 5 – During this time, the prophets Haggai and Zechariah encouraged the people.

6. Chapter 6 – King Darius decreed that the work should proceed unhindered.

7. Chapter 7 – After a fifty-eight-year gap, Ezra prepared to lead another group from Persia under the blessing of King Artaxerxes.

8. Chapter 8 – Ezra and his company journeyed and eventually arrived in Jerusalem.

9. Chapter 9 – Ezra wept and prayed for the nation because of their intermarriage with heathen.

10. Chapter 10 – Ezra's example of humble confession and prayer led to a national revival.

• An outline for Ezra is:

1. Restoration of the temple under Zerubbabel (chapters 1–6).

2. Reformation of the people under Ezra (chapters 7–10).

INTRODUCTION TO NEHEMIAH
The Building of the Walls

- Most Bible expositors agree that Nehemiah authored the book that bears his name. Nothing much is known about Nehemiah's childhood, youth, or family background, except that his father's name was Hachaliah (1:1) and his brother was Hanani (1:2).

- Nehemiah had risen to a position of prominence in his pagan environment. He was serving King Artaxerxes as his personal cupbearer (1:11). This position was a responsible one (certifying that none of the wine the king drank was poisoned) and an influential one (since such a trusted servant often became a close advisor).

- The book of Nehemiah records not only the physical rebuilding of the wall but also the spiritual restoration of the people. Nehemiah desired the approval of God more than the approval of people.

- Nehemiah was a man of prayer. Ten recorded prayers range from the quick "arrow prayer" (6:9) to the Bible's longest recorded prayer (9:5-38). There are prayers of confession and repentance, prayers of praise and adoration, prayers of supplication in weakness, and prayers for God's judgment on the enemies.

- God's hand of judgment fell on Israel because of their sin, which was characterized by idolatry and immorality. The northern kingdom fell to Assyria in 722 B.C. and the southern kingdom was taken into captivity in 786 B.C.. In 539 B.C., the power of Babylon was broken by the

Medes and Persians, and at that time many Jews returned to their homeland.

- Several years later, in 468 B.C., a second group of Jews returned, led by Ezra (Ezra 7:1–10). They found Israel in a bad state of spiritual and moral decline. The Jews had intermarried with the unbelieving peoples of the surrounding nations and were participating in their pagan practices. However, through Ezra's faithful teaching ministry, the majority of these people turned from their sins and once again followed God's will for their lives.

- Fourteen years after Ezra's return to Jerusalem, Nehemiah came on the scene and rebuilt the walls. He demonstrated unmatched skills in leadership and organization, and in fifty-two days the wall was completed.

- This book was the last recorded history of Israel in the Old Testament before the silent years.

- A suggested outline for the book is:

  1. The work of construction (chapters 1–7).
  2. The work of consecration (chapters 8–10).
  3. The work of consolidation (chapters 11–13).

INTRODUCTION TO ESTHER
The Queen Comes to the Rescue

- Although Esther follows Nehemiah in the Bible, its events are about thirty years prior to those recorded in Nehemiah

- Although no one knows who wrote this book, it was apparently written by a Jew living in Persia. He made use of records kept by Mordecai and could have used the records of the books of Chronicles.

- Drama, power, and romance describe a true story lived and written centuries ago in the book of Esther. This book gives us a segment of the history of the Jews that is not covered elsewhere in the Bible.

- The chief characters of the book are King Ahasuerus (another name for Xerxes), Vashti, Haman, Esther, and Mordecai. Although the name of God is not mentioned in the entire narrative, the book of Esther is a living illustration of the unseen hand of God's providence.

- Esther and Mordecai were living in the royal city of Susa. This city had been an important political, cultural, and religious center for centuries. At this time the city was one of the capital cities of a vast empire stretching from what is now India in the east to Turkey and Ethiopia in the west. In fact, the ruins of Susa are in Iran near its border with Iraq.

- The book of Esther begins with Queen Vashti refusing to obey an order from her husband, King Ahasuerus.

Because of this, she was removed and the search began for a new queen. Through a series of circumstances, a young Jewish woman by the name of Esther was brought to the palace and was chosen to become the new queen.

- At the same time, Mordecai, Esther's older cousin, became a government official. A man by the name of Haman was appointed second in command to the king. When Mordecai refused to bow in reverence to him, Haman became angry and determined to destroy Mordecai and all the Jews along with him.

- When Esther found out that Haman planned to destroy her people, she exposed him to the king. As a result, the king sentenced Haman to die on the gallows that he had built for Mordecai. Mordecai was promoted to Haman's position, and as a result, the Jews were guaranteed protection throughout the land and a whole nation was saved.

- A suggested outline is:

  1. How the plot was formed (chapters 1–3).
  2. How the plot was fought (chapters 4–5).
  3. How the plot was foiled (chapters 6–10).

INTRODUCTION TO JOB
From Riches to Rags and Rags to Riches

- The book of Job is named after its principal character, around whom the events of the narrative revolve. The name "Job" means persecuted one.

- The author of the book is unknown, but he was obviously a wise and well-educated man with literary skills. It is possible that Job wrote the book himself, after his restoration. Other suggested authors include Moses, Solomon, Hezekiah, Isaiah, Ezra, and Elihu.

- The period of the patriarchs seems to be the most likely time period for the book of Job. Job was not a descendant of Abraham, and he did not live in the land of Canaan. The text identifies his land as Uz.

- Job, the book, tells the story of Job, the man of God. It is a gripping story of riches to rags and then rags to riches. It tells how in a matter of minutes, a prominently wealthy and godly man lost all of his possessions, all of his children, and finally his health. Even his wife told Job to curse God and die, and his friends condemned rather than consoled him.

- Job was a prosperous farmer living in the land of Uz. He had thousands of sheep, camels, and other livestock. He also had a large family and many servants. Satan was allowed to destroy Job's children, servants, livestock, herdsmen, and home, but Job continued to follow God. Then he experienced extreme physical pain as he was covered with boils. Then his wife deserted him, and his friends told him to confess his sins and turn back to God. Finally, God spoke to him out of a whirlwind and Job fell in humble reverence before Him. In the end, Job was restored to happiness and wealth.

• This book wrestles with the age-old question as to why righteous men suffer if God is one of love and mercy. It is easy to think that we have the answers, but in reality, only God knows why things happen as they do. We can be sure that God is in control of every situation and only He understands why the good are allowed to suffer.

• This book also teaches that to ask why, as Job did (3:11–12, 16, 20), is not wrong. However, to demand that God answer why, as Job also did (13:22; 19:7, 31:15), is wrong. This constitutes a challenge as to God's sovereignty. The best question is to ask God *what* He wants us to learn through suffering rather than *why* it happened.

• The book can be outlined as follows:

1. The disasters of Job (chapters 1–2).
2. The friends of Job (chapters 3–37).
3. The conversation of Job with God (chapters 38–41).
4. The deliverance of Job (chapter 42).

INTRODUCTION TO PSALMS
God's Song Book

- Psalms means "book of praise songs" (this is the national hymn book of Israel).

- The Psalms are poems, and they are intended to be sung.

- This is the largest book in the Bible.

- There is a surprising similarity throughout the Psalms, and yet none are quite identical.

- David was the main writer of the Psalms, but he did not write all of them.

- The Psalms frequently refer to musical instruments, singing, and clapping in the religious activities.

- These poetic songs were a vital part of both the public and private worship of ancient Israel (II Chronicles 29–30).

- The early church quickly adapted the Psalms as part of their praise to God (Ephesians 5:19).

- It is believed that the Psalms were written over the course of many years, but they did not begin to be put together into a collection until the time of David.

- The Psalms came from a relatively few historical settings. Some were born during David's fugitive years in the days of Saul or during the rebellion of Absalom.

Others were written when David was firmly enthroned as Israel's king. A few were penned in the days of agony that followed his sin with Bathsheba. It is believed that Hezekiah wrote a small number of the Psalms during the Assyrian invasion. Some relate to the experiences of Israel during the Babylonian captivity and others to the hardships of returning to the Promised Land.

• It is a book of prayer and praise and is valuable as a manual, guide, and model for the devotional needs of the individual believer.

• The Qumran scrolls (found near the Dead Sea) show that the Psalms were divided into five volumes:

1. Book 1 – <u>Trust in times of testing</u> (chapters 1–41).
2. Book 2 – <u>Confidence in God stressed</u> (chapters 42–72).
3. Book 3 – <u>Resting in His mercy</u> (chapters 73–89).
4. Book 4 – <u>Assurance and praise</u> (chapters 90–106).
5. Book 5 – <u>Variety of themes</u> (chapters 107–150).

INTRODUCTION TO PROVERBS
Practical Wisdom for All Ages

- The book of Proverbs provides teaching in how to lead wise, godly lives and how to avoid the pitfalls of unwise and ungodly conduct.

- The book of Proverbs is different than any other book in the Bible. It is not history, poetry, prophecy, or law. It deals with such topics as wisdom, sin, goodness, wealth, temptation, pride, humility, justice, folly, friendship, idleness, poverty, family life, pleasure, revenge, strife, gluttony, drunkenness, and success.

- The key verse is "The fear of the Lord is the beginning of knowledge: but fools despise wisdom and instruction" (1:7).

- Solomon was the principal author of Proverbs according to I Kings 4:32. Solomon spoke three thousand proverbs, of which we have only one thousand in this book.

- He wrote three books of the Bible, but we do not know for sure the order in which they were written. It has been suggested that he wrote the Song of Solomon when he was young and in love, Proverbs when he was middle-aged and full of intelligence, and Ecclesiastes when he was old, disappointed, and disillusioned with the carnality of much of his life.

- Solomon was known as the richest and wisest man who ever lived, and yet as the years slipped away, he made some very sad and serious mistakes as he entered into political marriages with the daughters of pagan kings.

- The theme of the book is wisdom for living with specific instruction on such subjects as wealth, poverty, the tongue, pride, vengeance, strife, love, lust, laziness, friends, children, family, life, and death.

- Related thoughts are scattered throughout the book. Do not be surprised at the lack of grouping of concepts and that some of the things once said occur again and again in the same or varied form.

- Proverbs makes it clear that heavenly wisdom is priceless, virtue is blessed of God, and vice is always to be shunned.

- Proverbs stresses being rightly related to God and then being rightly related to others.

- The real problem in studying the book of Proverbs is to know where to start. The book contains 31 chapters and 915 verses, and almost every verse jumps to a different thought. This makes it impossible to outline the book.

INTRODUCTION TO ECCLESIASTES
The Royal Preacher

- This book centers on the philosophy of life: What is life? Why is life? Where is it going? and What am I supposed to do about it?

- The author of this book identifies himself as "the son of David, king in Jerusalem" (1:1, 12), although his name never appears in the book. All evidence seems to identify wisdom (1:16), unequaled wealth (2:7), and extensive building activities (2:4–6) that all point to Solomon.

- Although the tone of Ecclesiastes is generally negative and pessimistic, the entire book is filled with practical wisdom about how to accomplish great things in this world and stay out of trouble. It is also filled with spiritual wisdom concerning how to find and know eternal values. The writer affirms that righteousness is rewarded and wickedness is punished (8:12–13). However, the righteous are subject to the same unpredictable misfortunes as the wicked (9:1–2) and ultimately die just as the wicked do (9:3).

- At both the beginning (1:2) and the ending (12:8) of the book, the author declares that everything is "meaningless" or "vanity." This includes work (1:14), wisdom (2:15), righteousness (8:14), wealth (2:26), prestige (4:16), or pleasure (2:1–2). At the same time, life should not be filled with despair. True satisfaction comes from knowing that what we are doing is a part of God's purpose for our lives. This book helps us see that our scramble for power, approval, and money is useless, but our life should be lived in complete trust in God.

- Solomon's reign began under most promising conditions: "He loved the Lord, walking in the statutes of David his father.... They feared the king, for they saw that the wisdom of God was in him, to do judgment" (I Kings 3:3, 28). However, soon his own "wisdom" alone was guiding him. He openly ignored God by taking many wives, which consisted of heathen women. They seduced him into practicing idolatry (I Kings 11:1).

- Ecclesiastes makes it plan that human wisdom doesn't contain all the answers in life and that knowledge and education have their limits. To understand life, we need the wisdom that can be found only in God's Word (the Bible). To have God's wisdom, we must first get to know the Lord and honor Him. Solomon shows how empty it is to pursue the pleasures that this life has to offer rather than a relationship with the living Christ. The sure cure for emptiness is to center our thoughts on Christ and fill our lives with serving Him.

- A suggested outline for the book is:

  1. The preacher's subject (1:1–11).
  2. The preacher's sermon (1:12–10:20).
  3. The preacher's summary (chapters 11–12).

INTRODUCTION OF SONG OF SOLOMON
The Shulamite Love Story

- The Song of Solomon is Solomon's beautiful love song. It is a poem and a picture. It is an expression of love between a bride and her bridegroom. It describes real love as the love that makes one person willing to give up everything for the one he or she loves.

- This is perhaps one of the most difficult and mysterious books in the entire Bible. A research of material on this book will soon reveal that there is more diversity of opinions concerning it than perhaps any other book in the Bible.

- However, it is agreed by most Bible scholars that the author is Solomon. Some wonder how Solomon could be the author of a book that promotes faithfulness in marriage when he was so unfaithful with over seven hundred wives and three hundred concubines (I Kings 11:3). Perhaps the answer to this is that he wrote this "song" in his youth, before being overtaken by his own obsession with women.

- This book proves that God thinks sex is important, and Scripture contains numerous guidelines for its use and warnings about its misuse. The Song of Solomon gives an intimate story of a man and woman and their love, courtship, and marriage.

- It is interesting to note that of the more than one thousand songs Solomon wrote, only this one was designed by God to be included in the biblical canon.

- This is undoubtedly one of the most beautiful books in the Bible. The song abounds in imagery drawn from both country and urban life, and its language is full of vitality. It should be clear to anyone who reads it that the Holy Spirit intends for it to be a testimony to the true nature of God's love. It gives God's endorsement of marital love that is wholesome and pure.

- This moving story, drama, and poem features the love dialogue between a simple Jewish maiden (the Shulamite woman) and her lover (Solomon, the king). Some say it is an allegory of God's love for Israel and/or Christ's love for His bride, the church. Others say it is a literal story about married love, but in reality, it is probably both.

- Today's society has turned loving into lusting, giving into getting, and lasting commitment into a "no strings attached" philosophy. God thinks sex is important, and Scripture contains numerous guidelines for its use and warnings about its misuse.

- A broad outline for this book is:

  1. The beginning of love (chapters 1–4).
  2. The broadening of love (chapters 5–8).

INTRODUCTION TO ISAIAH
The Evangelical Prophet

• Isaiah was born into an influential, upperclass family that rubbed shoulders with royalty. He mentioned the name of his father, Amoz, seven times throughout the book. Amoz was a prominent citizen of Jerusalem. Isaiah was married and had two sons, Shear-Jashub and Maher-Shalah-Hash-Baz.

• Isaiah was called to his ministry "in the year that king Uzziah died" (6:1), which was 739 B.C. He had a long life span as he ministered throughout the reigns of Jotham, Ahaz, and Hezekiah, who died in 686 B.C.

• Tradition says that he was martyred during the reign of Manasseh by being sawed in two inside a hollow log. Isaiah was a man who loved his nation, hated sin and sham religion, and was in touch with God.

• The prophet announces judgment upon immoral and idolatrous people beginning with Judah, then Judah's neighboring nations, and finally the whole world.

• Isaiah was a prophet that not only wrote for his day but his message is one we also need to hear today as he cries out God's message in this world of upheaval, "Comfort ye, comfort ye my people" (40:1).

• The book can be outlined as follows:

1. Isaiah denouncing sin:

   a. The personal sins of the people (chapters 1–6).
   b. The national sins of the leaders (chapters 7–12).
   c. The sins of the Gentile nations (chapters 13–23.

2. A description of global judgment (chapters 24–27).

3. The impending Assyrian invasion (chapters 28–35).

4. God's miraculous deliverance of Jerusalem (chapters 36–37).

5. Hezekiah's foolish cooperation with Babylon (chapters 38–39).

6. A focus on the attributes of the Godhead:

   a. The greatness of God the Father (chapters 40–48).
   b. The grace of God the Son (chapters 49–57).
   c. The glory of God the Holy Spirit (chapters 58–66).

INTRODUCTION TO JEREMIAH
The Weeping Prophet

- Jeremiah is one of the five books of the Major Prophets, which are called "major" primarily from the standpoint of the length of the prophecies.

- Jeremiah was often called the weeping prophet (9:1; 13:17). He began his ministry (at about the age of twenty) under good King Josiah, with whom he enjoyed cordial relations. However, after Josiah's death, opposition mounted. He barely escaped arrest and was forbidden to go to the temple.

- Jeremiah spoke to the nation of Judah during its hardest times. His contemporaries during this time were Habbakuk and Zephaniah (to Judah), Ezekiel and Daniel (to Babylon), and perhaps Nahum (to Nineveh).

- In 722 B.C., the northern kingdom of Israel was taken into captivity, which was about one hundred years before Jeremiah began to preach to Judah. Jeremiah began his prophetic ministry in the thirteenth year of Josiah's reign and continued through the reigns of Jehoahaz, Jehoiakim, Jehoiachin, and Zedekiah. He also prophesied during the occupation by Nebuchadnezzar and the exile in Egypt. Jeremiah's ministry covered about fifty years, and he apparently died in Egypt.

- Jeremiah was called by God to warn the people of Judah (the southern kingdom) of impending judgment. The theme that runs throughout the book is that of judgment against Judah. Because of idolatry, the people deserved the punishment of God. Even in his call it was evident to Jeremiah that his message would be one of condemnation rather than salvation (1:10, 18, 19). The people completely rejected not only the message, but the man as well. He was considered a traitor and was persecuted by the mighty and the lowly alike.

• It is helpful to realize that the book of Jeremiah does not follow the order in which things happened. Jeremiah and his assistant, Baruch, wrote Jeremiah's messages on a long scroll. Some Bible scholars have suggested that probably, while writing down one message, Jeremiah would be reminded of another message he had spoken before. The earlier message would then be added to the scroll where he had left off writing. This mixing of early and late messages makes it very difficult to know the order in which his messages were given.

• It has been said that Jeremiah was the simplest and grandest of the Old Testament prophets.

• A simple outline for the book:

1. The call of Jeremiah (chapter 1).
2. Prophecies to Judah (chapters 2–45).
3. Prophecies to the Gentiles (chapters 46–51).
4. The fall of Jerusalem (chapter 52).

INTRODUCTION TO LAMENTATIONS
The Desolate City

- The author of Lamentations is unnamed in the book, but internal and external evidence is consistently in favor of Jeremiah.

- The historical background of Lamentations can be found in the book of Jeremiah. It was written soon after Jerusalem's destruction (Jeremiah 39:52) at the beginning of the exile, somewhere around 586 B.C. Jeremiah probably wrote the book before he was taken captive to Egypt by his disobedient countrymen (Jeremiah 43:1–7).

- Lamentations is perhaps the saddest book of the Old Testament. It was penned by the mourning prophet Jeremiah after the fall of Jerusalem. His sorrow is obvious in his vivid descriptions of the defeat, destruction, and desolation of Jerusalem.

- There appear to be three themes that run through the five chapters of this book:

  1. Mourning over Jerusalem's holocaust.
  2. Confession of sin and acknowledgment of God's righteous judgment.
  3. Hope in God's future restoration of His people.

- Defeat, slaughter, and ruination, which had been promised for so long and were frequently ignored, were now being carried out by the brutal Babylonians. Yet as the prophet was heartbroken, he paused to proclaim a ringing testimony of deep faith in the goodness and mercy of God.

- In the face of death and destruction, with life seemingly coming apart at the seams, Jeremiah turned tragedy into a triumph of faith.

- The weeping prophet Jeremiah is a type of Christ who wept over the same city six centuries later (Matthew 23:37–38). Like Christ, Jeremiah identified himself personally with the plight of Jerusalem and with human suffering caused by sin.

- Lamentations includes elements that typify Christ's life and ministry as the Man of Sorrows who was acquainted with grief. He was afflicted, despised, and derided by His enemies.

- A suggested outline for the five chapters of this book:

  1. <u>Destruction of Jerusalem</u> (chapter 1).
  2. <u>Anger of God</u> (chapter 2).
  3. <u>Prayer for mercy</u> (chapter 3).
  4. <u>Siege of Jerusalem</u> (chapter 4).
  5. <u>Prayer for restoration</u> (chapter 5).

INTRODUCTION TO EZEKIEL
The Exiled Prophet

• The author of this book, Ezekiel, was a Jewish priest and a prophet who was exiled in Babylon. He ministered during the darkest days of Judah's history: the seventy-year period of Babylonian captivity.

• The fall of Jerusalem and the Babylonian exile were used by God to correct the sins of the people and draw them back from their sinful way of life. Ezekiel warned them that not only was the nation responsible for sin, but each individual was also accountable to God.

• Although he was a priest and prophet, he served as a Jewish "street preacher" in Babylon for twenty-two years. There he warned everyone about God's judgment and called them to repentance and obedience.

• Ezekiel is a book of visions, poems, parables, and comic street theater. However, to get the people's attention, God uses more than Ezekiel's vivid images and symbolic actions.

• If "thirtieth year" in chapter 1, verse 1, refers to Ezekiel's age, he was twenty-five years old when he was taken to Babylon and thirty when he received his prophetic commission (1:2–3). This means that he was about seventeen when Daniel was deported in 605 B.C., and they would have been about the same age.

• Ezekiel was a younger contemporary of Jeremiah. While Jeremiah ministered to the people still in Judah, Ezekiel prophesied to those already exiled in Babylon after the defeat of Jehoiachin. While Jeremiah delivered a chilling message of destruction in Jerusalem, Ezekiel brought a warming message of reconstruction in Babylon.

• Jeremiah was a man of tears while Ezekiel was a man of visions. Those visions stretched from horror to hope: from condemnation upon Judah's faithless leaders and godless foes to consolation regarding Judah's future.

• Ezekiel's twofold theme was condemnation (1–32) and consolation (33–48). He surveyed the sins that were bringing God's judgment and exposed the foolishness of their false hopes of an early return to the homeland. He then comforted them by assuring them of God's covenant promise of future blessing and complete restoration.

• A suggested outline for the book is:

1. Judah's fall: Before the siege (chapters 1–24).
2. Judah's foes: During the siege (chapters 25–32).
3. Judah's future: After the siege (chapters 33–48).

INTRODUCTION TO DANIEL
The Gentile Prophet

• Daniel the author was a statesman in the court of heathen monarchs, and throughout his life he was uncompromising and faithful to his God.

• He was taken captive as a youth to Babylon by Nebuchadnezzar in 605 B.C. He spent the rest of his life there as a government official and as a prophet of the true God.

• He was given a place of prominence and responsibility in Nebuchadnezzar's kingdom, was made one of three presidents under Darius (6:1), and lived until the third year of Cyrus.

• In Ezekiel 14:14 and 20, he is classified with Noah and Job as being one of the godliest of men.

• The basic message of the book deals with that period that our Lord called "the times of the Gentiles" (Luke 21:24).

• It contains two principal divisions: history (chapters 1–6) and prophecy (chapters 7–12). The sections have been called the "Historic Night" and the "Prophetic Light."

• Among the doctrines mentioned in the book are:

1. Personal separation (1:8; 3:12; 6:10).
2. Angels (8:16; 9:21).
3. Resurrection (12:2).
4. Antichrist (7:24–25; 9:27).

- Favorite stories in this book include those of Shadrach, Meshach, and Abednego (chapter 3); and Daniel in the lions' den (chapter 6).

- It seems that Daniel died in the first year of King Cyrus, and he may have helped inspire the decision of Cyrus to have the temple rebuilt (II Chronicles 36:22).

- The book is chiefly about the man Daniel and his message. Nothing finer could be recommended to the youth of today than a study of the life of Daniel.

- A suggested outline for the book:

  1. Daniel's background (chapter 1).
  2. Daniel interprets others dreams (chapters 2–7).
  3. An angel interprets Daniel's dreams (chapters 8–12).

INTRODUCTION TO HOSEA
The Broken Home Prophet

- This book tells a story of a man's love for his unfaithful spouse. But the story of the prophet Hosea and his wife Gomer illustrates another love story, and that is that God loves us, even when our sins have broken His heart. Here is a picture of God who longs to forgive us when we turn to Him.

- It is a story of one-sided love and faithfulness between a prophet and his faithless wife and Jehovah and His faithless people. Just as Gomer was married to Hosea, Israel is married to God. In both cases, the bride plays the harlot and runs after other lovers. But unconditional love keeps seeking even when it is spurned. Hosea offers the possibility of salvation if the nation will only turn from idolatry back to God.

- According to chapter 1, verse 1, the author of this book was Hosea, son of Beeri. It was probably written around 715 B.C. and recorded events from 753–715 B.C. Hosea began his ministry during the end of the prosperous but morally declining reign of Jeroboam II, king of Israel. He prophesied until shortly after the fall of Samaria in 722 B.C.

- The theme of the book is God's steadfast love for Israel in spite of her continued unfaithfulness and illustrates this through his marital experience. God told Hosea to find a wife, and told him ahead of time that she would be unfaithful to him. In obedience to God, Hosea married Gomer. After Hosea's marriage, as predicted, Gomer left him to pursue her lusts (chapter 2). But Hosea found her, redeemed her, and brought her home again, fully reconciled (chapter 3).

- Hosea's message to Israel can be summarized in three words: sin, judgment, and salvation. In exposing Israel's sin, Hosea emphasized its idolatry. He compared Israel's covenant relationship to the Lord with marriage and accused Israel of spiritual adultery. To illustrate Israel's infidelity, Hosea married a woman who would, like Israel, prove unfaithful to her husband.

- Just as Hosea went after his unfaithful wife to bring her back, so the Lord pursues us with His love. His love is tender, loyal, unchanging, and undying. As we read this book, we can see Hosea submit himself willingly to the Lord's direction, grieve with him over the unfaithfulness of his wife and his people, and hear the clear warning of judgment.

- The book of Hosea is organized according to two tragedies:

1. The tragedy in Hosea's home life (chapters 1–3).
2. The tragedy in Hosea's home land (chapters 4–14).

INTRODUCTION TO JOEL
The Prophet of the Plague

- The author was Joel, "the son of Pethuel" (1:1), who some think was a priest because of his repeated references to the priesthood of his day. However, such reasoning is by no means conclusive.

- It was apparently written during the days of young King Joash, who was under the surveillance of priests when he ascended to the throne of Judah at the age of seven (II Kings 11:21).

- Joel prophesied primarily to the two southern tribes, the kingdom of Judah.

- The prophecy was given because of a severe drought and an invasion of locusts, which Joel saw as a punishment for the sins of the people.

- The terrible locust plague that had recently occurred in Judah was used by Joel to illustrate the coming Day of Judgment when God will directly intervene to vindicate righteousness.

- Although Obadiah was the first prophet to mention the Day of the Lord (Obadiah 15), Joel was the first to develop this important biblical theme.

- This brief book of Joel develops the crucial theme of the coming Day of the Lord. It is a time of awesome judgment upon the people and the nations that have rebelled against God. However, it is also a time of future blessing upon those who have trusted in Him.

- Joel was written as a warning to the people of Judah of their need to humbly turn to the Lord with repentant hearts (2:12–17) so that God could bless rather than buffet them.

- The prophet dwells upon God's dealing in history, past and future, as a summons to sinners to abandon their iniquity and walk in righteousness.

- This description of a literal plague of locusts and its comparison with future judgments is a dramatic and literary gem.

- The purpose of Joel's prophecy is to turn the nation back to God in preparation for the coming great Day of the Lord.

- A suggested outline for the book:

  1. The Day of the Lord in *retrospect*: Past judgment on Judah (chapter 1).
  2. The Day of the Lord in *prospect*: Future judgment and restoration of Judah (chapters 2–3).

INTRODUCTION TO AMOS
The Country Preacher

- The only place the name Amos appears in the Old Testament is in this book. The name means "burden" or "burden-bearer." He lived up to the meaning of his name by bearing up under the burden of declaring judgment to rebellious Israel.

- Amos wrote this book at a time of economic growth and prosperity. Business was booming and boundaries were bulging, but below the surface, greed and injustice were festering.

- This book gives us God's perspective on some social issues. It tells us how God feels when the wealthy and the powerful exploit the poor and the defenseless. Amos spoke passionately about God's concern for the poor and he urged a returning to the Lord.

- The leadership and military conquests of Jeroboam II had enabled Israel to flourish. But while everything seemed fine on the surface, the moral fiber of the nation was disintegrating.

- This message was for the people of Israel, the northern kingdom. Amos was from Judah, the southern kingdom, and he challenged their materialism and low morality that they learned from their pagan neighbors. His prophecy was God's last appeal to Israel, warning them to repent before it was too late.

- Amos came from the rural area of Tekoa in Judah, twelve

miles south of Jerusalem, where he tended a special breed of small sheep that produced wool of excellent quality.

- He prophesied "in the days of Uzziah king of Judah, and in the days of Jeroboam the son of Joash king of Israel" (1:1). He anticipated the 722 B.C. Assyrian captivity of Israel (7:11).

- The basic theme of the book is the coming judgment of Israel because of the holiness of God and the sinfulness of His covenant people. God graciously sent Amos as a reformer to warn the people of their fate if they refused to repent. But they rejected his plea, and the course of judgment could not be altered.

- A clear anticipation of Christ is found at the end of the book. He has all authority to judge (1:1–9:10), but He will also restore His people (9:11–15).

- A suggested outline for the book consists of four divisions:

    1. Eight prophecies (chapters 1–2).
    2. Three sermons (chapters 3–6).
    3. Five visions (chapters 7–8).
    4. Five promises (chapter 9).

INTRODUCTION TO OBADIAH
Servant of the Lord

• It is not certain who Obadiah was or when he prophesied. He was an obscure prophet who probably lived in the southern kingdom of Judah. Nothing is known of his hometown or family, but it is not likely that he came out of the kingly or priestly line, because his father is not mentioned (1:1).

• This book gives an example of how a neighbor has taken advantage of a situation and gotten away with it. Obadiah tells how God will take care of such injustices.

• It is the shortest book in the Old Testament with only twenty-one verses, but it carries one of the strongest messages of judgment in the Old Testament.

• There are about twelve different Obadiahs in the Old Testament, and there is nothing to say for certain that he is any one of these.

• Although there is no conclusive evidence, it is thought by some that the Edomites were responsible for burning the Jerusalem temple.

• There is clear evidence of hostility between Judah and Edom from the time of David, around 1000 B.C. (II Samuel 8:13–14), right through the monarchical period. This fighting and feuding all began between twin brothers Esau and Jacob (Genesis 27).

• When Judah was invaded and conquered by Babylon,

Edom not only cheered and gloated, but they also looted Judah in the aftermath. They even captured those who tried to escape and turned them over to the enemy.

• Edom has become a symbol of all that stand in opposition to God.

• The major theme of Obadiah is a declaration of Edom's coming doom because of its arrogance and cruelty to Judah.

• It appears that Obadiah was a contemporary of Elisha and was one of the earliest of the writing prophets, predating Joel by a few years.

• A simple outline for Obadiah is:

1. Defeat of Israel: Judgment of Edom (1:1–18).
2. Victory of Israel: Restoration of Israel (1:19–21).

INTRODUCTION TO JONAH
The Unwilling Prophet

• Jonah, the son of Amittai, came from the tribe of Zebulon in the northern kingdom of Israel and was from the village of Gath-hepher, located about two miles northeast of the city of Nazareth. Nothing is known of Jonah, except what is learned about him from this book and a brief statement made about him in II Kings 14:25.

• Nineveh was located on the east bank of the Tigris River, about 550 miles from Samaria, capital of the northern kingdom. It was protected by a wall fifty feet wide and one hundred feet high.

• This book was probably written sometime between 785 and 750 B.C., which was during the reign of Jeroboam II as king of Israel. Israel's northern kingdom was restored by Jeroboam II. At the same time, the Assyrians, whose capital city was Nineveh (a city of 120,000), were flaunting their power before God and the world through numerous acts of heartless cruelty. It is said that this capital of Assyria was the largest city in the world in that day and was a definite threat to the existence of Israel. So, when Jonah heard God tell him to go to Assyria and call the people to repentance, he ran in the opposite direction.

• Jonah hated the Assyrians, and he wanted vengeance and not mercy. Because of this, he ran the other way. However, God had a job for Jonah to do, so he caused him to change his mind after spending three days in the fish's belly. After this, Jonah decided to obey God. He preached in the streets for Nineveh, and the people repented and were delivered from judgment. At this point, Jonah sulked because God didn't bring judgment on the people.

• As you read Jonah, you can see the full picture of God's love and compassion and realize that no one is beyond redemption. It is great to know that the Gospel is for all who will repent and believe (II Peter 3:9).

• Jonah is the only prophet that Jesus likened to Himself (Matthew 12:39–41). Jonah's experience is a type of the death, burial, and resurrection of Christ.

• It is interesting to note that of all the things mentioned in this book—the storm, the lots, the sailors, the fish, the Ninevites, the plant, the worm, and the east wind—only the prophet himself fails to obey God

• A suggested outline for the book is:

1. Running from God: Disobedient prophet (chapter 1).
2. Running to God: Disciplined prophet (chapter 2).
3. Running with God: Docile prophet (chapter 3).
4. Running behind God: Disgruntled prophet (chapter 4).

INTRODUCTION TO MICAH
The Prophetic Prophet

• Micah was a contemporary of Hosea and Isaiah—Hosea in the northern kingdom and Isaiah in the court of Jerusalem.

• Micah's hometown of Moresheth-gath (1:14) was located about twenty-five miles southwest of Jerusalem on the border of Judah and Philistia. Like Amos, he was from the country. He was also called to be a prophet and to deliver a stern message of judgment to the people of Jerusalem.

• He prophesied during a period of intense social injustice in Judah. False prophets preached for riches. Princes thrived on cruelty, violence, and corruption. Priests ministered more for greed than for God. Landlords stole from the poor and evicted widows. Judges lusted after bribes. Businessmen used deceitful scales and weights. Sin had influenced every segment of society, and a word from God was very appropriate.

• All of the things above led to an increasing gap between the rich and the poor. The poor were oppressed with no recourse to the courts because of corrupt judges, so Micah took up their cause. He drew a sharp contrast between this "pop religion" and true faith, which involves justice, mercy, and walking humbly with God (6:8).

• These prophecies were given during the reigns of Jothan, Ahaz, and Hezekiah (1:1). After the prosperous reign of Uzziah in Judah, his son Jothan came to power and followed his father's policies. He was basically a good king, although he failed to remove the idolatrous high places. Under the wicked king Ahaz, Judah was threatened by the forces of Assyria and Syria. Hezekiah opposed the Assyrians and successfully withstood their invasion with the help of God. He was an unusually good king who guided the people back to a relationship with God.

- About one-third of the book exposes the sins of Micah's countrymen, another third predicts the judgment that will come as a result of those sins, and the final third holds out the hope of restoration once the discipline has ended.

- The book closes on a note of hope. The same God who executes judgment also delights in giving mercy. He does not retain His anger forever, because He delights in mercy (7:18).

- A suggested outline for the book is:

  1. Prediction of judgment: Punishment (chapters 1–3).
  2. Prediction of restoration: Promise (chapters 4–5).
  3. Plea for repentance: Pardon (chapters 6–7).

INTRODUCTION TO NAHUM
The Prophet of Doom

* Nahum is seventh of the Minor Prophets.

* Nothing is known about the author of this brief prophecy except that he was Nahum the Elkoshite.

* Elkosh was probably a village in Galilee. Some say it was the city that later was named Capernaum.

* The subject of this prophecy is Nineveh (1:1). A heavy-weight of doom, a burden rested on the Assyrian capital. Several other Old Testament passages refer to Assyria's fall.

* Nineveh was situated on the east bank of the Tigris River. Sennacherib fortified the city's defensive wall whose glory, he said, "overthrows the enemy.

* The author's references to the destruction of No (3:8–10), which took place in 664 B.C., and his predic-tion of Nineveh's doom when it fell to the Babylonians in 612 B.C., seem to place the writing of the book during this fifty-two-year intervening period.

* Nimrod went to Assyria and built Nineveh (Genesis 10:8–10) around 2300 B.C.

* Shalmaneser III (859–824 B.C.) made the city of Nineveh a base for military operations.

* Jonah preached to the Ninevites between 772–754 B.C.

- Nineveh was the capital of one of the cruelest, vilest, most powerful, and most idolatrous empires in the world. Nahum called Nineveh "the bloody city" (3:1), which was noted for its "inequity" (2:12)!

- When Nahum prophesied, Judah was under the Assyrian yoke (1:13, 15; 2:1, 3).

- The purpose of Nahum's book is to announce the fall of Nineveh and thereby comfort Judah with the assurance that God is still in control.

- We could outline Nahum as follows:

1. The certainty of God's judgment (chapter 1).
2. The description of God's judgment (chapter 2).
3. The reasons for God's judgment (chapter 3).

INTRODUCTION TO HABAKKUK
The Problem Prophet

• Nothing is known about the author, Habakkuk. Someone has said, "Who he was, nobody knows; what he was, everybody knows."

• The fact that the prophet is known to us only by name once again indicates the relative unimportance of the prophet and the major importance of the prophecy, and more importantly, the God who gave us the prophecy.

• Some have inferred that Habakkuk was a Levite who assisted in the music of the temple. The concluding note in his book, "To the chief singer on my stringed instruments" (3:19), suggests that Habakkuk may have been a musician of the Levitical office.

• The date of Habakkuk's prophecy is difficult to ascertain, for he does not mention the king or kings during whose reigns he prophesied. Most commentators, however, date Habakkuk's prophecy as being during the reign of King Jehoiakim, who was a godless king that led his nation down the path of destruction.

• However, we do know that when Habakkuk prophesied, the southern kingdom was wallowing in its sin and tottering politically in view of the impending danger of Babylon, the current world power. Nebuchadnezzar had already carried Daniel and many of Jerusalem's nobles into captivity (606 B.C.), and this second deportation was soon to follow (597 B.C.).

- The prophecy of Habakkuk is unique among all of prophetical literature. The first two chapters constitute a dialogue between the prophet and Jehovah concerning the invasion of the Chaldeans (1:1–11) and the destruction of the Chaldeans (1:12–2:20). Chapter 3 contains instructions given to the musicians (3:1, 19). In the first two chapters the prophet contends with Jehovah, and in the third he submits to Jehovah.

- Habakkuk is a unique book. Unlike other prophets who declared God's message to people, this prophet dialogued with God about people.

- Habakkuk wrote in a time of international crisis and national corruption. Babylonia had just emerged as a world power. A new empire was stretching across the world. Soon the Babylonians would overtake Judah and carry its inhabitants away into captivity. On the eve of impending destruction, a period of uncertainty and fear, Habakkuk wrote his message.

- A suggested outline for the book is:

  1. Problems of Habakkuk: Warn of coming judgment (chapters 1–2).
  2. Praise of Habakkuk: Comfort amidst ultimate destruction (chapter 3).

INTRODUCTION TO ZEPHANIAH
The Royal Prophet

• Beyond this book that bears his name, very little is known about the author, Zephaniah. His ancestry is traced back four generations, which is unique among the prophets. His lineage shows that he was the great-great grandson of good King Hezekiah. If so, he was the only prophet of royal descent.

• By giving his lineage and citing King Josiah, who was a distant relative, he linked himself with the godly kings and godly remnants of Israel's history. Josiah was the God-fearing son of Amon, who together with his father Manasseh were two of the most wicked kings of Israel's history (II Kings 22–23).

• Despite King Josiah's well-intended civil and religious reforms, leaders were corrupt and idolatry was widespread. The Assyrian empire, the superpower that had ruled over Judah for more than a century, was disintegrating. Shortly after Josiah's death and Zephaniah's ministry, the Babylonians conquered Judah, destroyed the temple, and took many into exile.

• Zephaniah wrote to the people of Judah warning them of impending judgment for their sins. He hoped to stir them to repentance before it was too late. At the same time, it seems that Zephaniah intended to encourage the followers of the Lord by assuring them that God would preserve a remnant and ultimately fulfill His promises to their forefathers.

- Zephaniah is a book of contrasts, for no other prophet painted a blacker picture of God's judgments or a brighter picture of Israel's future glory. The theme of the book is the impending judgment of God on Judah for its disobedience. On the other hand, he pointed out God's steadfast and everlasting promise to protect His people.

- Upon the backdrop of describing the judgments of God on Judah, Zephaniah went further than any of the other minor prophets in emphasizing the full conversion of the Gentiles to the worship of the true God. Historically, it is thought by many that this book was used in the providence of God to prepare the nation for the reforms and revival under King Josiah.

- When justice is distorted, when the line between right and wrong is blurred, or when leaders become corrupt, it is easy to become discouraged. Zephaniah reassures us that we can still trust God, and even in dark times our faith can still burn brightly.

- The suggested outline for this book is:

1. Judgment on Judah (1:1–3:8).
2. Restoration for Judah (3:9–3:20).

INTRODUCTION TO HAGGAI
A Call to Build

- Haggai is the second shortest book in the Old Testament; only Obadiah is shorter.

- Haggai is thought to have been about eighty years old when he prophesied, which may have been a factor that accounts for his very brief ministry. The entire book covers only a four-month span.

- This book is set in the context of the return of the Jews from the Babylonian exile and the subsequent rebuilding of Jerusalem and the temple. Sixteen years after the rebuilding began, the people had yet to finish the project because their personal affairs had God's business. Only twenty-three days after his first oracle, the people began to work on the temple for the first time.

- It was through the ministry of Haggai (along with Zechariah) that the rebuilding of the temple progressed (see Ezra 5:1–2). Haggai was a contemporary of Zechariah. He was the practical doer, while Zechariah was the visionary.

- This book records not only the oracles of Haggai, but also his ministry and the response of the people to it. He preached a fiery series of sermonettes designed to stir up the nation to finish the temple. He called the builders to renewed courage in the Lord, renewed holiness of life, and renewed faith in God who controls the future.

- He called the builders to renewed courage in the only

thing that proves that a man belongs to God, which is the righteousness of his life. But what is righteousness? John's Gospel is clear and unequivocal on this subject: to be righteous is to love our brothers. That, says John, is a duty about which we should never be in any doubt (John 15:12,13).

• Haggai and Malachi were two minor prophets who addressed key issues faced by both the church and the home today. Included in their books are such things as attitudes, priorities, the use of money, the problem of divorce, and the second coming of Christ.

• Apart from the book that bears his name, Haggai is mentioned only in Ezra 5:1 and 6:14.

• The name Haggai means "feast" or "festival," which usually refers to the three pilgrimage feasts (Feasts of Unleavened Bread, Weeks, and Tabernacles) of the Jewish religious calendar. It has been suggested that he may have been born during one of these festive celebrations.

• An outline for the book:

1. The temple of God (1:1–2:9).
2. The blessings of God (2:10–2:23).

INTRODUCTION TO ZECHARIAH
The Visionary Prophet

* The prophet Zechariah was a Levite born in Babylon (Nehemiah 12:1, 16). He was the son of Berechiah and the grandson of Iddo the priest (Zechariah 1:1). Ezra and Nehemiah referred to him as "a descendant of Iddo" (Ezra 5:1, 6:14; Nehemiah 12:4, 16), implying perhaps that his father had died young and Zechariah became the successor of his grandfather (Nehemiah 12:4, 16).

* Zechariah returned to Jerusalem from Babylon with almost fifty thousand other Jewish exiles. He was probably a relatively young man at the beginning of his prophetic ministry (2:4) while Haggai might have been considerably older.

* This book is named after its author, Zechariah, who was a contemporary of Haggai the prophet, Zerubbabel the governor, and Joshua the high priest. Like Jeremiah and Ezekiel before him, Zechariah was both a prophet and a priest.

* Zechariah was a younger contemporary of Haggai and continued the ministry that he began. Both men ministered to the same people, but from different perspectives. Haggai reproved the people for their failure to rebuild the temple, while Zechariah encouraged the people by presenting them prophecies concerning Christ.

* Zechariah was one of the most devotional writers of the Old Testament. He dwelt more completely on the person and work of Christ than any of other prophetic writings.

- Zechariah was probably born in Babylon during the seventy-year Babylonian captivity. After these seventy years, the people had been granted the king's permission to return to their land and rebuild their beloved capital city, Jerusalem (Ezra 1:2–3). However, many of them felt very comfortable in Babylon and did not want to risk leaving that land for pioneer work.

- As a result, only a minority had returned under the leadership of Zerubbabel, but this returning remnant was filled with burning enthusiasm. Within seven months they had rebuilt the altar, and soon afterward they had started to rebuild the temple.

- The theme of the book is rebuilding the temple and the nation of Judah. It also covers the Lord's return.

- A suggested outline for the book is:

  1. <u>Pictures</u>: Eight visions (chapters 1–6).
  2. <u>Problems</u>: Four messages (chapters 7–8).
  3. <u>Predictions</u>: Two burdens (chapters 9–14).

INTRODUCTION TO MALACHI
The Last of the Prophets

- Written by Malachi (1:1), the last of the Old Testament prophets.

- Written to the nation of Israel (1:1).

- Malachi, a prophet in the days of Nehemiah, directed his message of judgment to a people plagued with corrupt priests, wicked practices, and a false sense of security in their privileged relationship with God.

- The book of Malachi marks the close of Old Testament prophecy and the beginning of four hundred years of silence between the Old and New Testaments.

- Using a question and answer format, Malachi highlighted Judah's hardheartedness and pronounced God's curse upon all who would practice such things

- These were all the Jewish people who returned to Jerusalem under Zerubbabel after the Babylonian captivity (Ezra 1) in 536 B.C.

- Malachi was a contemporary of Nehemiah. The books of Nehemiah and Ezra give the history of events taking place during this time.

- Malachi rebuked the priests for malpractice in the temple (chapter 2). This is evidence that the temple had been rebuilt and was being used (3:10). The temple was completed and dedicated in 515 B.C. (Ezra 6:15–16).

- The fact that the people of Israel were unfaithful in their worship of God suggests that considerable time had passed since the temple was completed. For these reasons, most scholars agree that this book was written around 450–430 B.C., or one hundred years after the Jews had returned to Palestine. Evidences of their unfaithfulness are:

1. They were unwilling to part with money for temple funds (3:8).
2. They took advantage of the poor, the strangers, the orphans, and the widows (3:5).
3. They were intermarrying with Gentiles who followed other gods (2:11).

A suggested outline:

1. Care of God: Past (chapter 1:1–5).
2. Complaint of God: Present (chapters 1:6–3:15).
3. Coming of God: Future (chapters 3:16–4:6).

INTRODUCTION TO MATTHEW
The King of Kings

- This book was written twenty or thirty years after Jesus had gone back to heaven. It was written for Jewish readers to answer the questions they had about Jesus (24:2).

- The book was written by Matthew, a publican (tax collector) for the Roman government who lived in Capernaum and was surnamed Levi (Mark 2:14). Publicans were despised by fellow Jews.

- Matthew described Jesus as the Doer and the Teacher. He recorded at least twenty specific miracles and six major messages: the Sermon on the Mount (chapters 5–7), the charge to the apostles (chapter 10), the parables of the kingdom (chapter 13), the lesson on forgiveness (chapter 18), and the prophetic discourse on the Mount of Olives (chapters 24–25).

- Matthew did not write to tell us about himself, but instead, he gave us the words and works of Jesus. In fact, we do not find a single recorded word that he spoke.

- Matthew's gospel is saturated with Old Testament quotations, containing some sixty references.

- The Old Testament ended with God's people looking for their long-promised King, their Messiah. Matthew's gospel shows that Jesus was that King, and thus the theme of the book is Christ the King.

- Matthew's gospel is the bridge that leads us out of the

Old Testament and into the New Testament.

• Being a Jew, Matthew fully understood the Jewish messianic hope, and his gospel is designed to convince his own nation that the long-awaited Messiah is none other than Jesus.

• The genealogy of Christ, ending with Joseph, the foster father of Jesus, is given by Matthew.

• The Olivet Discourse (chapters 24–25) is one of the most concise yet comprehensive prophetic passages in the Bible.

• Matthew, Mark, and Luke present much similar material about the life of Christ, and thus are called the Synoptic Gospels.

• The closing verses record the Great Commission to go into all the world.

• Outline for Matthew:

  1. Offering of the King (chapters 1–10).
  2. Rejection of the King (chapters 11–28).

INTRODUCTION TO MARK
The Master Servant

• This book was written by the son of a well-to-do lady in Jerusalem whose name was Mary. Her house was the meeting place of the early church (Acts 12:12).

• Mark's gospel is the shortest of the four gospels and presents the Lord Jesus as the suffering servant.

• Mark was the nephew of Barnabas who went with Paul on their first missionary journey. When they reached Perga, for some reason he decided to return home (Acts 14:14).

• When Paul and Barnabas were planning their second missionary journey, Barnabas wanted to take Mark again, but because of his quitting the first journey, Paul said no. This caused a division between Paul and Barnabas, but later from prison, Paul sent for Mark when he said, "Take Mark, and bring him with thee: for he is profitable to me for the ministry" (II Timothy 4:11).

• The book of Mark is the oldest and the shortest of all the gospels, and it is believed that it was written after Peter died.

• This is a biography of Jesus Christ; however, it does not dwell on His early childhood but launches right into His ministry.

• Almost forty percent of this gospel is devoted to a detailed account of the last eight days of Jesus' life, climaxing in His resurrection.

- Mark stressed the supernatural work of Jesus' ministry as he described nineteen miracles while giving only four parables.

- To Mark, Jesus was not simply a man among men; He was God among men. None of the other gospels gives such a human picture of Jesus.

- Early church tradition says that Mark wrote this gospel in Rome, and that is why he did not give Jewish genealogy as the other gospel writers did. This would have been of less concern to the Roman mind.

- An outline of the book (Jesus as servant):

  1. <u>Service</u>: Life and ministry of Jesus the servant (chapters 1–13).
  2. <u>Sacrifice</u>: Death and resurrection of Jesus the servant (chapters 14–16).

INTRODUCTION TO LUKE
The Perfect Man

- This book was written by Luke, "the beloved physician" and often companion of Paul. He is thought by many to have been the only Gentile author of any part of the New Testament.

- Luke was a tremendous historian, missionary, church planter, traveler, and writer, as well as a physician.

- Luke gave the most complete account of Christ's ancestry. He wanted to create an accurate, chronological, and comprehensive account of the unique life of Jesus Christ to strengthen the faith of Gentile believers and stimulate saving faith among nonbelievers.

- Though specifically dedicated to Theophilus, this gospel is slanted toward all Gentiles. Theophilus was apparently a high official of some sort.

- Luke's emphasis was on the humanity of Christ. Twenty-six times the key phrase "Son of Man" is found in the gospel as he attempted to present an accurate account of the facts about the life of Christ.

- The key word of Luke's gospel is "save." Together with the forms "Savior" and "salvation," the word is used twenty times in the book.

- More than half of the material found in this gospel is not in any of the other three. Luke included more than the other gospels about women, children, the home, the Holy

Spirit, prayer, and praise.

- Although Matthew is divided into more chapters, Luke is actually the longest and most comprehensive of the four gospels, presenting Jesus as the perfect Man who came to seek and to save lost sinners.

- All the gospels except John's were written before the destruction of Jerusalem in A.D. 70. The precise place where Luke penned his gospel is not known, but some speculate that it may have been in Caesarea during Paul's two-year imprisonment there (Acts 24:27). It covers the time period from the announcement to Zacharias to the ascension of Christ.

- An outline of the book (presenting Jesus as the Son of Man):

1. Seeking the lost (chapters 1–18).
2. Saving the lost (chapters 19–24).

INTRODUCTION TO JOHN
Master Teacher

- The writer of this gospel is identified in the book only as "the disciple whom Jesus loved" (21:7). However, most Bible scholars agree that it was the Apostle John.

- John was the son of Zebedee, who was a master fisherman, and Salome, one of the women who ministered to the Lord.

- He apparently came from a fairly well-to-do home (Mark 15:40–41); just the fact that he had a home of his own in Jerusalem (19:27) was evidence that he was in comfortable circumstances.

- John wrote his gospel some thirty or forty years after the other gospels had been written; thus, he did not feel it necessary to repeat many of the details that had already been given.

- The first part of this gospel concentrates on Jesus' public ministry and the "signs" that reveal who He really is. The second part shifts from the crowds to the disciples and Jesus' private ministry among them.

- This gospel contains no parables, but instead it focuses on seven miracles (five of which are not recorded elsewhere) that reveal the Father's glory in the Son:

- Its key word is "believe," which occurs ninety-eight times in this book. Jesus is presented as the one whom we are to believe.

- John with his brother James obeyed the call of Jesus (Mark 1:20). It would seem that James and John were in partnership with Peter in the fishing business (Luke 5:7–10). He was one of the inner circle of the disciples.

- This fourth gospel has the clearest purpose statement in the Bible: "But these are written, that ye might believe that Jesus is the Christ, the Son of God; and that believing ye might have life through his name" (20:31).

- An outline as suggested by Bruce Wilkinson:

  1. Introduction to Christ (1:1-18).
  2. Revelation of Christ (1:19-4:54).
  3. Rejection of Christ (5:1-12:50).
  4. Revelation from Christ (13:1-17:26).
  5. Crucifixion and Resurrection (18:1-21:25).

INTRODUCTION TO ACTS
History of Missions

- The book of Acts is a history book of the church and is the chief source for the facts concerning Christianity in the first century after Christ.

- Although Luke is nowhere named within the book, it is agreed by most Bible scholars that Luke, "the beloved physician" (Colossians 4:14), was the author.

- The general theme is getting the Gospel into all the world through the power of the Holy Spirit, beginning in Jerusalem and from there spreading into Judea, Samaria, and the uttermost part of the world (1:8).

- The book covers the period of time from the resurrection of Christ to Paul's first imprisonment at Rome, which would be approximately thirty-three years.

- This has been charted in the book *The Acts of the Apostles* by Barclay as follows:

  1. The church in Jerusalem (1:1–6:7).
  2. From Jerusalem to Palestine (6:8–9:31).
  3. From Palestine to Antioch (9:32–12:24).
  4. From Antioch to Asia (12:25–16:5).
  5. From Asia to Europe (16:6–19:20).
  6. From Europe to Rome (19:21–28:31).

- Acts furnishes us the principles for revival and missionary work. We need to go to the epistles, and not the book of Acts, for our doctrine.

- It should be noted that the Bible is arranged with the life of Jesus on one side of Acts and the letters of the apostles on the other.

- Acts can be divided as follows:

  1. Gospel taken primarily to the Jews (chapters 1–12).

     a. Peter is the chief character.
     b. Jerusalem is the central city.

  2. Gospel preached to the Gentiles (chapters 13–28).

     a. Paul is the principal character.
     b. Antioch is the main city.

INTRODUCTION TO ROMANS
A Doctrinal Treatise

- Warren Wiersbe writes, "The Epistle to the Romans was not written for religious sightseers. You will have to think as you study this letter, but the rewards will be worth the efforts."

- It appears that Paul wrote this letter during a three-month visit in Corinth at the home of a friend and convert by the name of Gaius (Romans 16:23).

- After fulfilling a mission of mercy in Jerusalem, Paul had planned to travel to Spain, stopping en route for a visit in Rome, the capital of the then known world. However, his plan did not work as he intended. Instead of going as a tourist, he went as a prisoner, where he remained under house arrest for at least two years.

- With Paul's Hebrew religion, his Greek education, and his Roman citizenship, he was well prepared for the great work God had for him to do as well as the suffering he had to face.

- The central theme throughout the book is that salvation is a gift that cannot be earned but can only be received by faith. Paul contrasts this theme against the teaching of certain Jewish legalists who wanted to add circumcision to grace.

- The book of Romans begins by presenting the picture of the guilt all men share, and then presents God's answer to man's unhappy predicament.

- It appears that there was not one central church in Rome but there were several assemblies meeting in private homes. One of these was in the house of Aquila and Priscilla. Therefore, the letter is not addressed to the church at Rome, but to all the faithful in Rome.

- It has been said that Romans is the most fundamental, vital, logical, profound, and systematic discussion of the whole plan of salvation in all the literature of the world. It touches all men: it is universal in its application and its roots are not only in man's creation and fall, but also in the timeless purposes and decrees of God.

- Paul clearly outlined the foundations of the Christian faith: all people are sinful; Christ died to forgive sin; we are made right with God through faith; this begins a new life with a new relationship with God. If we study Romans carefully, we will never be at a loss to know what to believe and how to behave.

- The book of Romans can be divided as follows:

1. What to believe (chapters 1–11).
2. How to behave (chapters 12–16).

INTRODUCTION TO I CORINTHIANS
Problem Solving

• I Corinthians was written by Paul from Ephesus to a church largely made up of Gentiles.

• The city of Corinth lies fifty miles west of Athens on a narrow neck of land between the Aegean and Adriatic Seas. It was a crossroads for travel and commerce.

• Corinth contained a number of pagan temples including Aphrodite's, which was visible far out to sea. This temple was serviced by a thousand slave girls who doubled as temple prostitutes and as entertainers for the city night life.

• This, the longest of Paul's letters, deals with the quarrels and questions of the Corinthian church. This was a gifted church but was carnal, worldly, and childish.

• This book gives you God's perspective on some very hot topics as it reveals the humanity of Christians and shares how Paul dealt with rumors, factions, and fights in the church. The church that operates on the principles in this book can have an impact on today's world.

• No other epistle gives a better look at problems and conditions in an apostolic church. The wide variety of subjects discussed is easy to follow because of its logical development.

• The Gospel was first preached in Corinth by Paul on his second missionary journey. Upon arrival in the city, Paul accepted the hospitality of Aquila and Priscilla who were exiled Jews from Rome. During the week he worked with them making tents (Acts 18:1–4), and on the Sabbath he reasoned with the Jews in the synagogue concerning Christ.

- Paul's letter to the Corinthians was brought about by at least two factors. First, he had received word from two sources concerning problems that included divisions in the church (1:11) and immorality (5:6–9:20). Second, he received a letter from the assembly requesting answers to a series of questions concerning marriage, food, worship, and the Resurrection.

- Paul wrote this letter to address their problems, heal their divisions, and answer their questions. He confronted them with their sin and their need for corrective action and encouraged them to make a clear commitment to Christ. We could summarize his discussion into two categories: unsolicited advice (chapters 1–6 and 15) and solicited advice (chapters 7–14).

An outline for the book:

1. Concern: Divisions in the church (chapters 1–4).
2. Condemnation: Disorder in the church (chapters 5–6).
3. Counsel: Difficulties in the church (chapters 7–16).

INTRODUCTION TO II CORINTHIANS
Critics Answered

• Paul probably wrote his first letter to the Corinthians in the spring of the year and his second one before winter in the same year.

• II Corinthians 1:1 indicates that this letter was to be shared with other believers in the Roman province of Achaia.

• Corinth had a reputation for prosperity, but she was also a byword for evil living. It was the place where the Isthmiasn Games were held, which were second only to the Olympics.

• This book is an outpouring of the Apostle Paul's heart toward a group of believers in a church that he had founded and that he dearly loved.

• On Paul's second missionary journey he had visited Corinth, a city in the southwest corner of Greece, where he preached the Gospel and spent eighteen months establishing the church.

• Later, Paul had written a letter (I Corinthians) to them in which he dealt with grave and pressing problems confronting the church.

• We cannot be sure of all that took place between I and II Corinthians, but it seems that Paul made a visit to Corinth and found that the problems that occasioned the first letter had not been solved (13:1–2). Following this visit he wrote the church a severe and sorrowful letter (2:4), which in all probability was lost in its entirety.

- After receiving word from Titus the good news that the church had repented, Paul wrote this letter from Philippi (in Macedonia), hoping to visit them again soon (12:14).

- Keep in mind that these Corinthian believers were subjected to persecution from enemies without and to treachery from enemies within their group.

- Few passages in the Bible so clearly present the case for sacrificial giving as 8:1–9:15 does.

- As we read this intensely personal letter, we need to listen to Paul's words of love and exhortation and his commitment to the truth of the Word of God.

- A suggested outline:

    1. <u>Paul and his commission</u> (chapters 1–5).
    2. <u>Paul and his converts</u> (chapters 6–9).
    3 <u>Paul and his critics</u> (chapters 10–13).

INTRODUCTIONS TO GALATIANS
Christian Liberty Explained

* It was written in an emergency. False teachers were trying to mix law with grace as a condition of salvation. In other words, they taught it was faith plus works. This theological problem threatened the very existence of these infant assemblies. These false teachers were saying that to really be saved, a person must generally "keep the law of Moses" (Acts 15:5) and especially "be circumcised" (Acts 15:1).

* The Apostle Paul did not open this letter in his usual fashion of praise to God and prayer for the saints. He jumped right in with both feet, condemning the error and admonishing the believers to turn back to the purity of the Gospel.

* It was probably written during Paul's third missionary journey and not addressed to just one assembly but "the churches of Galatia" (1:2). No other book (except perhaps Romans) so forcefully points out that we are saved by believing and not by achieving.

* The location of the Galatian churches was in central Asia Minor, which is now modern Turkey. These churches were founded by the Apostle Paul on his first missionary journey (Acts 13:1–14) and included such places as Antioch, Iconium, Lystra, and Derbe.

* This book warns of a popular substitute for spiritual living that we find in many churches today: that people think they are "spiritual" because of what they do or

don't do, because of the leader they follow, or because of the group they belong to.

• In the doctrinal section of this book are some arguments that are hard for us to understand. However, the main point of the entire letter is very clear. Paul returned again and again to one central question: Are we saved by what we do or by what Christ has done for us?

• Every verse and every argument in this book ultimately makes its way back to that core issue. It's faith versus works, or grace versus the Law of Moses. The very heart of the Gospel is at stake in these words penned by the Apostle Paul.

• Paul explains how the Galatians were beginning to turn from faith to legalism. This struggle between the Gospel and legalism is still prevalent today.

• This short letter has three parts:

1. The personal section: The Gospel of grace defended (chapters 1–2).
2. The doctrinal section: The Gospel of grace explained (chapters 3–4).
3. The practical section: The Gospel of grace applied (chapters 5–6).

INTRODUCTION TO EPHESIANS
Preventing Problems in the Church

- Paul was a prisoner at the time he wrote this letter (Ephesians 3:1; 4:1; 6:20).

- He was probably under house arrest in Rome. Tychicus delivered this letter to the Ephesians (Ephesians 6:21–22).

- Ephesians is classified as one of the prison epistles along with Philemon, Philippians, and Colossians.

- Ephesus was situated about three miles from the Aegean Sea and had a population of approximately 340,000.

- It was famous for its rich culture, Oriental religion, Greek philosophy, Roman government, and worldwide commerce.

- Ephesus was noted for the Great Temple of Diana and was the capital of heathen worship.

- The temple of Diana was 425 feet long and 220 feet wide and was known as one of the seven wonders of the world. It contained a beautiful stadium seating twenty-five thousand.

- Paul made a brief visit to Ephesus at the end of his second missionary journey, but on his third missionary journey he remained there for about three years while they experienced a great revival.

- During this time, many people turned to Christ from worshiping the great Ephesian goddess. This really upset Demetries the silversmith, who had a thriving business making shrines of Artemis. He called a meeting of the other craftsmen. Because of fear of losing their business, they banded together and drove Paul out of town.

- This letter was written to a group of believers who were rich in Christ but were living like beggars because they were ignorant of their wealth. The Christian's heavenly bank account is made up of adoption, acceptance, redemption, forgiveness, wisdom, and inheritance.

- A simple outline for the book is:

  1. <u>Belief</u>: Privileges of the Christian (chapters 1–3).
  2. <u>Behavior</u>: Responsibilities of the Christian (chapters 4–6).

INTRODUCTION TO PHILIPPIANS
How to Have Real Joy

- Philippines is often referred to as the letter of joy. The words "joy" and "rejoicing" are used eighteen times throughout the book. The words "sin" and "sins" are not found in this epistle. In fact, we find no murmuring or complaining. Paul finds joy as he prays for the people in their tribulation (1:4). Happiness depends on happenings, but joy depends on Christ.

- The book was written to the church at Philippi by Paul while he was in prison in Rome. In obedience to the Macedonian call, Paul had taken the Gospel to Philippi on his second missionary journey. There was no synagogue there, so he met with interested people at the riverside. As a result, a church was established, which was the first church in Europe.

- At the time of this writing, Epaphroditus had brought a contribution to Paul from the church in Philippi (4:18). While he was in Rome, he became so ill he almost died (2:27). When he was well enough, Paul sent him back with this letter of thanks and an explanation of Epaphroditus' long absence.

- The unusual thing about this letter is that Paul's situation was such that there appears to be no reason for him to be rejoicing. He was a Roman prisoner, chained to a Roman soldier, and was not permitted to preach in public. His case was coming up shortly, and there was a possibility he might even be beheaded. Yet, in spite of his circumstances, Paul was filled with joy.

- The initial reason for Paul writing this book was to thank the Philippians for their love gift. However, he also took advantage of this opportunity to address some of the problems in the church. Those included rivalries (2:3–4), the teaching of the Judaizers (3:1–3), perfectionism (3:12–14), antinomian influence that was creeping in (3:18–19), and personal ambitions (4:2).

- The Philippian believers had enjoyed a very special relationship with Paul, so he wrote them a personal expression of his love and affection. They had brought him great joy (4:1).

- Paul's desire to know Christ above all else is wonderfully expressed in 3:8–9: "Yea doubtless, and I count all things but loss for the excellency of the knowledge of Christ Jesus my Lord: for whom I have suffered the loss of all things, and count them but dung, that I may win Christ, and be found in him."

- The outline that Warren Wiersbe gives to this epistle is as follows:

  1. Joy in spite of circumstances (chapter 1).
  2. Joy in spite of people (chapter 2).
  3. Joy in spite of things (chapter 3).
  4. Joy that defeats worry (chapter 4).

INTRODUCTION TO COLOSSIANS
Error Dealt With

- This letter was written by Paul while he was imprisoned at Rome.

- In the first two chapters, we find what Christ did *for us,* and in the last two chapters we find what Christ does *through us.*

- The first half of the book is doctrinal and the second half is practical. It shows how Christ needs to be first in everything and that the Christian life should reflect that priority.

- The purpose of this letter was to refute error in the church. Some believers were attempting to combine elements of paganism and secular philosophy with Christian doctrine.

- The error against which Paul warned in this book later became known as Gnosticism.

- There is no record that Paul had ever been to Colossae, but he was well acquainted there.

- Epaphras seems to have been the one who established the church at Colossae (1:6–7). He was one of Paul's co-laborers and was probably converted in Ephesus during Paul's stay there.

- The city of Colossae was located about one hundred miles west of Ephesus in a district of Asia Minor (now modern Turkey).

- This city was built along the Lycus River and was one of three population centers that flourished in that region. Laodicea and Hieropolis were the other two cities.

- This letter was delivered to the church by Tychicus and Onesimus (4:7–9), who also took letters to the Ephesians and Philemon (Ephesians 6:21).

- This letter contains great doctrines of the Gospel and was to be read aloud in the churches.

- It seems that the Colossian church was composed mainly of Gentile converts (1:21; 2:11, 13).

- This letter shows how relationships inside and outside the home should demonstrate daily the transformation that faith in Jesus Christ makes in the walk of the believer.

- A simple outline for the book is:

  1. The truth about Christ (chapter 1).
  2. The truth about cults (chapter 2).
  3. The truth about Christians (chapters 3–4).

INTRODUCTION TO I THESSALONIANS
The Lord's Coming

- I Thessalonians is among the earliest of all New Testament writings. It was written by the apostle Paul, probably around 51 A.D. from Corinth.

- Paul had established the church in Thessalonica during his second missionary journey (Acts 17:1–9) and wrote this letter a short time later.

- Paul and his companions were faithful to bring the Gospel to the Thessalonians in the midst of persecution. The Thessalonians had only recently become Christians and yet remained faithful to the Lord, despite the fact that the apostles were not yet with them.

- The purpose of the letter was to strengthen the Thessalonian Christians in their faith and give them the assurance of Christ's return.

- Thessalonica, named after Alexander the Great's half sister, was a great and important city located on the Egnation highway. Since this was a great commercial highway, Thessalonica became a place for the wealthy to live; however, the majority of the people made their living by manual labor.

- Thessalonica was one of the most important centers of population in Paul's day, occupying a strategic location both governmentally and militarily. It was the prominent seaport and capital of the Roman province of Macedonia.

- Thessalonica was also a free city, which meant its citizens enjoyed autonomy in all of its internal affairs.

- We do not know how long Paul stayed in Thessalonica, but we do know he was there long enough to gain employment (Philippians 4:16) and to receive two gifts of money from the Philippians.

- Paul presented the great doctrine of the Rapture of the Church (chapter 4), and because of this, it was a great source of encouragement to the Thessalonians, and is to us today as well.

- This is a letter from a pastor who was basically satisfied and even thrilled with the progress of his flock. The church at Thessalonica was in many ways a model church.

- A brief outline of the book includes:

  1. Personal experience: Looking back (chapters 1–2).
  2. Practical exhortation: Looking forward (chapters 3–5).

INTRODUCTION TO II THESSALONIANS
The End Times

- Paul reminded the Thessalonians of the events that must take place before Christ returns.

- This is the shortest of Paul's nine letters to the churches, but it provides crucial information concerning the end times and clarifies issues that would otherwise be very obscure.

- This letter was also written by Paul, who wrote I Thessalonians under the inspiration of the Holy Spirit (I Thessalonians 1:1). Twice the writer refers to himself as Paul (1:1; 3:17).

- Like the first epistle, II Thessalonians was written in Corinth to the church at Thessalonica and to all believers everywhere..

- It is primarily a letter of correction:

  1. Concerning persecution (chapter 1).
  2. Concerning prophecy (chapters 2 and 4).
  3. Concerning practice (chapter 3).

- Paul had heard about conditions in the church. Many had interpreted Paul's first letter to say that the Second Coming would be at any moment. Because of this misunderstanding, many of the people persisted in being idle and disorderly with the excuse of waiting for Christ's return.

- Paul commended his children in the faith for their growth, corrected their error in doctrine about the Day of the Lord, and warned of its consequences. In this letter, Paul indicated various events that must precede the second coming of Christ.

- The imminent coming of Christ should never cause us to be idle; we should be even more busy, using our time wisely and working for Him while we wait. The doctrine of the Lord's return requires a balance between waiting and working. It is a perspective that should encourage holiness, not idleness.

- As we read II Thessalonians, we see clearly the reality of the Lord's return and our responsibility to live for Him until that day.

- The following is a suggested outline of the book:

  1. Encouragement in persecution: Thanksgiving for their lives (chapter 1).
  2. Explanation of the Day of the Lord: Instruction in their doctrine (chapter 2).
  3. Exhortation to the church: Correction of their behavior (chapter 3).

INTRODUCTION TO I TIMOTHY
Qualifications for Leadership

- Written by Paul (1:1), an experienced apostle.

- Written to Timothy (1:2), a young pastor facing responsibility in the church at Ephesus. He was the son of a Gentile father and a Jewish mother (Acts 16:1).

- His mother Eunice and grandmother Lois were Jewish believers who helped to shape his spiritual life (II Timothy 1:5).

- As a child, he knew and believed the Hebrew Scriptures (II Timothy 3:15) but was led to the Lord possibly by Paul himself (1:2).

- He became one of Paul's closest companions, and to him Paul addressed two of his three pastoral letters.

- Timothy was in Ephesus where Paul had recently asked him to stay and provide leadership for that congregation (1:3). He was to appoint elders, combat false doctrine, and supervise church life as an apostolic representative.

- Paul was hoping to soon visit Timothy, who faced all sorts of pressures, conflicts, and challenges from the church and his surrounding culture. However, to counsel and encourage Timothy, Paul sent this very personal letter (3:14).

- Apparently Timothy had physical problems (5:23).

- This letter, in the meantime, would guide Timothy in his pastoral responsibilities so that his flock would know how to behave as a church (3:14–15).

- Paul listed character qualities for leadership, demonstrating how true leadership comes from our walk with God rather than from achievements or vocational success.

- We might say that I Timothy is a handbook of church administration and discipline.

- A suggested outline for the book:

1. Warning: Dangers of false doctrine (chapter 1).
2. Worship: Directions for worship (chapters 2–3).
3. Wisdom: Defense against false teachers (chapter 4).
4. Widows: Duties toward others (chapter 5).
5. Wealth: Dealings with riches (chapter 6).

INTRODUCTION TO II TIMOTHY
Exhortations to Sound Doctrine

- This was Paul's last letter to Timothy. It was written as a farewell, urging Timothy to come to him. He longed to see his young son in the faith once more before he died.

- It is referred to as a "prison epistle" because it was written while Paul was a prisoner in a Roman dungeon.

- Not long after he wrote this, he was beheaded.

- It was written to encourage Timothy in his ministry at Ephesus. Knowing Timothy's natural timidity, Paul was concerned that the threatening prospects should not overwhelm him.

- He instructed Timothy in how to carry on after he was gone.

- In A.D. 64, a great fire destroyed a large part of the city of Rome. Rumors circulated that the fire had been ordered by Nero himself.

- In a desperate effort to clear himself, Nero blamed the Christians for starting the fire, and hundreds of Christians were put to death.

- II Timothy was probably written following the edict of Nero against the Christians.

- The primary theme of this letter is being "a good soldier" (2:3). This can be accomplished only through faithfulness in the face of hardship.

• Paul elaborated on the coming apostasy and sought to prepare the Lord's servants for times of testing to come.

• At the time of this writing, Paul was held in a damp, cold prison cell, under the sentence of death, or at least was expecting that sentence any day.

• No other book in the Bible has so many instructions concerning pastoral care.

• A suggested outline for the book is:

1. The *call* of a good soldier (chapter 1).
2. The *character* of a good soldier (chapter 2).
3. The *caution* of a good soldier (chapter 3:1–13).
4. The *conditioning* of a good soldier (chapter 3:14–17).
5. The *commands* of a good soldier (chapter 4:1–5).
6. The *comfort* of a good soldier (chapter 4:6–22).

INTRODUCTION TO TITUS
Local Church Organization

• Titus was apparently a Greek convert who had been won to Christ through Paul's personal ministry (Titus 1:4).

• Like Timothy, he was probably a young man, but unlike Timothy, he was not given to timidity and physical ailments.

• Early in his Christian life, Titus had accompanied Paul to Jerusalem to discuss the relationship of the Gentiles to the Law of Moses. Paul used Titus as a test case, refusing to allow him to be circumcised despite the insistence of the Judaizers.

• As a trusted colleague of Paul's, Titus was sent to deliver his second letter to the Corinthians and was also given the responsibility of arranging for the collection to be given to the poor in Jerusalem.

• It seems that Paul then left him on the Island of Crete to help in the organizing of churches. Crete is a large island in the Mediterranean, southwest of Greece.

• In this letter to Titus, Paul reminded him to appoint good leaders who would guide the church wisely. He also urged Titus to combat the false teachers found on the island.

• Titus is very similar to I Timothy with its instructions to pastors.

- Paul expressed great confidence in Titus, calling him "my partner" (II Corinthians 8:23).

- Paul called for church order and right living on an island known for laziness, gluttony, lying, and evil. We need to take heed in obeying this message in our day when discipline is not respected or rewarded by our society.

- An outline of the book (practical wisdom concerning church organization and administration):

  1. Church organization (chapter 1).

     a. Leaders must be chosen on the basis of proven character and conduct.
     b. False teachers must be quickly detected and removed.

  2. Church obligation (chapters 2–3).

     a. Speak sound doctrine.
     b. Maintain good works.

INTRODUCTION TO PHILEMON
The Runaway Slave

- Paul was a prisoner in Rome when he wrote to Philemon. Therefore, it is often referred to as one of the "prison epistles."

- It is a personal note written to a friend about a private matter.

- This letter was written to Philemon, who was evidently a wealthy resident of Colossae who had a home large enough to house the local church (v. 2).

- Paul had evidently led Philemon to the Lord when he ministered in that area a few years before, and they had become good friends.

- Paul's letter to Philemon is a masterpiece of diplomacy and tact in dealing with a festering social sore in the Roman empire: human slavery.

- Slavery was very common in the Roman Empire, and evidently some Christians had slaves.

- Onesimus was a domestic slave of Philemon who was a member of the church in Colossae. He had run away and evidently robbed his master when he left (v. 18).

- He made his way to Rome and somehow came in contact with Paul, who led him to the Lord.

- Paul convinced Onesimus that running from his problems

wouldn't solve them, and he persuaded Onesimus to return to his master.

• There were approximately sixty million slaves in the Roman Empire when Paul wrote this letter.

• Roman law that governed slavery in that day considered slaves nothing more than property to be bought and sold and even beaten or killed if they did not obey. It is with this background in mind that we find Paul sending Onesimus, as a fugitive, back to his master Philemon.

• Paul's intercession for Onesimus illustrates what Christ has done for us. As Paul interceded for a slave, so Christ intercedes for us who are slaves to sin. As Paul offered to pay the debts of a slave, so Christ paid our debt of sin.

• Outline of Philemon (the runaway slave and his master):

1. Paul's praise of Philemon (vv. 1–7).
2. Paul's plea for Onesimus (vv. 8–17).
3. Paul's pledge to Philemon (vv. 18–22).

INTRODUCTION TO HEBREWS
Patterns for Living

• This book was written by an unknown human author. Many have been suggested, but probably the favorite choice has been Paul, perhaps because the King James translation lists him as author.

• Even though no one knows for sure who the human author was, we do know that, as with all Scripture, it was inspired by God.

• Neither do we know the exact date it was written. However, many Bible scholars say that it must have been written after Christ's ascension, which was about A.D. 30, and before the destruction of Jerusalem in A.D. 70.

• Also, we do not know what particular assembly it was addressed to, but whoever these people were, it is clear that they had suffered great persecution (10:32–34).

• It is called the book of Hebrews simply because the early church was at first exclusively composed of Hebrews. There are no references to Gentiles in the book.

• Some say this book was written exclusively to Christians, warning them of the danger of losing their salvation. Another group teaches that the people addressed were not truly born-again believers, but merely professing Christians who had come only part way to Christ. It seems to me that perhaps it was written to a church, much like we may attend today, where there were born-again Christians, professing Christians, and those who didn't profess anything.

- Because of persecution, many of these Jewish believers thought it might be better to go back to Judaism. The writer of Hebrews exhorted them to "press on" to maturity in Christ.

- The following appeals were made to these believers based on the superiority of Christ over the Judaic system:

  1. Christ is better than the angels, for they worship Him (1:4-2:18).
  2. Christ is better than Moses, for Moses was created by Him (3:1-4:13).
  3. Christ is better than the priesthood, for His sacrifice was once for all time (4:14-7:28).
  4. Christ is better than the Law, for He mediates a better covenant (8:1-13).

- An outline for the book is:

  1. Superiority of Christ's way (1:1–4:13).
  2. Superiority of Christ's work (4:14–10:18).
  3. Superiority of the Christian's walk (10:19–13:25).

INTRODUCTION TO JAMES
The Marks of Spiritual Maturity

* It was written by James (1:1). Possibly it was the first New Testament book to be written.

* James was the half-brother of Jesus Christ (Matthew 13:55–56; John 7:2–5; I Corinthians 15:7; Acts 1:14). He did not become a follower of Jesus until after Jesus rose from the dead.

* He was a key leader of the Jerusalem church (Acts 21:15–19; Galatians 2:9; Acts 12:16–17).

* He moderated the first church conference (Acts 14:27–15:33). This council approved Gentiles becoming a part of the church.

* It was probably written prior to the Jerusalem council held in A.D. 50.

* It was written to scattered Jewish believers living outside Palestine (1:1–2). Many of the Jewish believers were being persecuted for their faith in Christ.

* These Jewish Christians were having problems in their personal lives, and all of these problems had a common cause: spiritual immaturity. James wrote to them about how to face their difficulties and live the Christian life.

* Because these scattered people were believers in Jesus Christ, they had been rejected by their nation and their own Jewish families. They were also rejected as foreigners

in strange lands with strange gods.

- This letter could be considered a how-to book on Christian living, confrontation, and challenge, as well as a call to commitment.

- What James had to say is very practical. He emphasized that Christianity is a living faith—a faith that works (2:14–26). A good question for us to ask ourselves each day as we read the passage is, "If we say that we believe as we should, then why do we behave as we shouldn't?"

- James encouraged his readers to patiently endure the sufferings of this present life in view of the future prospect of the coming of the Lord (5:7–12).

- The marks of a spiritually mature Christian are covered in this outline:

  1. He is patient in testing (chapter 1).
  2. He practices the truth (chapter 2).
  3. He has power over the tongue (chapter 3).
  4. He is a peacemaker (chapter 4).
  5. He is prayerful in troubles (chapter 5).

INTRODUCTION TO I PETER
A Message of Hope

- This letter was written by Simon Peter. Peter was the nickname given to Simon by Jesus when they first met. He is the only man in the New Testament by this name.

- It is directed specifically to Christians scattered in the region of present-day Turkey. Five Roman provinces are mentioned: Pontus, Galatia, Cappadocia, Asia, and Bithynia.

- Written in "Babylon" (5:13). Some think this refers to a city on the Euphrates River, while others think it was a city in Egypt, but most think it was probably Rome, which is referred to elsewhere in Scripture as Babylon.

- As we study I Peter, we will see how the three themes of suffering, grace, and glory unite to form an encouraging message for believers experiencing times of trial and persecution.

- Peter, son of Jonas, left a fishing business with his brother, Andrew, to follow Jesus. They had a home in Capernaum at the time.

- Regardless of what any religious groups may say, we know that Peter was married because of the reference to his mother-in-law in Mark 1:30.

- I Peter was written at a time when it was extremely dangerous to declare one's personal faith in Jesus as Savior and Lord. Christianity had been outlawed, and

Nero was doing all he could to eradicate the "sect" from his empire.

• Important events in Peter's life include:

1. Walking on water (Matthew 14:22–36).
2. His confession of faith (Matthew 16:13–23).
3. His boast that he never would forsake Christ, followed by his denial (Matthew 26:31–35).
4. Repentance (Matthew 26:75; John 21:15–24).
5. Sermons at the Pentecost and after healing the lame man (Acts 2 and 3).
6. Deliverance by an angel from imprisonment and execution (Acts 12).
7. Preaching to the Gentiles (Acts 10).
8. Testimony for salvation through faith and for Christian liberty at Jerusalem (Acts 15).
9. Denial of Christian liberty by his actions at Antioch (Galatians 2).

• Warren Wiersbe offers this as one way to outline I Peter:

1. God's grace and salvation (1:1–2:10).
2. God's grace and submission (2:11–3:12).
3. God's grace and suffering (3:13–5:11).

INTRODUCTION TO II PETER
Standing Firm in Truth

- I Peter deals with problems from the outside (persecution from unbelievers); II Peter deals with problems from the inside (defection from within the church).

- Although Peter did not name the location from which he wrote his second letter, it was probably written from Rome.

- Peter knew that his time on earth was limited (1:13–14), so he wrote about what was on his heart, warning believers of what would happen after he was gone, especially about false teachers and the unchanging truth of the Gospel.

- A clear biblical description of the divine-human process of inspiration is found in chapter 1, verse 21: "But holy men of God spake as they were moved by the Holy Ghost."

- Tradition states that Peter was crucified in Rome during the persecutions of Nero sometime in late A.D. 67 or early A.D. 68, when he was approximately seventy-five years old.

- It seems to have been written to both Jewish and Gentile Christians.

- It was written to warn the believers against false teachers who would enter the flock. These teachers were proud of their position, promoted sexual sin, and advised against keeping the Ten Commandments

- There is strong evidence that the Apostle Peter wrote II Peter himself.

- II Peter is a very important book for the twentieth century because it deals with the very issues we need to be reminded of today. These are:

  1. We need to remain firm in the truth given to us by the prophets and our Lord (chapter 1).
  2. We need to be warned about those who lead us away from the word of truth (chapter 2).
  3. We need to be reminded that the world will one day end when the Lord returns (chapter 3).

- Those who scoff at the thought of future judgment will find, like Sodom and Gomorrah, that ignoring God's Word will ultimately lead to destruction! The warning for believers is clear in Chapter 3: "Be not ignorant" (v. 8), "be diligent" (v. 14), and "beware" (v. 17).

- The book can be outlined as follows:

  1. Cultivation of Christian character: Holiness (chapter 1).
  2. Condemnation of false teachers: Heresy (chapter 2).
  3. Confident of Christ's return: Hope (chapter 3).

INTRODUCTION TO I JOHN
Back to the Basics

• John, the beloved disciple and a member of Jesus' intimate company of three, was the author of this epistle. He also wrote II and III John as well as the gospel of John.

• John was a fisherman when Jesus called him to be one of His followers. His mother Salome was probably a sister of Mary, Jesus' mother, which would make him a cousin of Jesus.

• This book was probably written from Ephesus to the Christians who were scattered all over Asia Minor.

• It was written primarily for believers. It was written at a time when the first days of Christianity had become a thing of habit—the first thrill was gone and the flame of devotion had died to a flicker.

• The purpose of this epistle is stated in I John 1:3–4: "That which we have seen and heard declare we unto you, that ye also may have fellowship with us: and truly our fellowship is with the Father, and with his Son Jesus Christ."

• What he wrote is as appealing as how he wrote. The Apostle John wrote to meet needs, and what he wrote is right on target with what God wants you to know and apply.

• John's object in writing this book is at least five-fold:

1. To promote fellowship (1:3).

2. To produce happiness (1:4).
3. To protect holiness (2:1).
4. To prevent heresy (2:26).
5. To provide hope (5:13).

- John had two great things to say about God in this book:

  1. "God is light, and in him is no darkness at all" (1:5).
  2, "God is love" (4:8), and that caused Him to love us before we loved Him.

- A possible outline is:

  1. Living in God's light (chapters 1–2).
  2. Living by God's love (chapters 3–4).
  3. Living with God's life (chapter 5).

INTRODUCTION TO II JOHN
Walking in Truth

• This is the second shortest book in the Bible (III John is slightly shorter).

• There was no question in the minds of the church fathers who lived closest to the time of John that these three epistles (I, II, and III John) were written by the apostle.

• John wrote this perhaps to accompany his more general letter (I John). He may have hoped it would renew commitment to the truth by further exposing the false teachers.

• This is a brief personal letter by the Apostle John to "the elect lady" (the church).

• The book was written that we might know how to deal with heretics. John's warning is stern, but he knew that a letter is not the best place to go into detail, so he promised to deal more fully with the problem when he would come for a personal visit.

• It warns that people who do not hold to Bible teaching about Christ are not saved.

• John commended love as a necessary ingredient of the Christian life, but it must be discerning. It must not blindly embrace those who willfully seek to destroy the truth.

• It is false love that opens the door to false teaching. John even warned the people not to receive into their house anyone who rejected the teaching of Christ. Biblical love is a matter of choice; it is dangerous and foolish to float through life with undiscerning love.

- All three of John's letters develop the theme of fellowship:

  1. I John focuses on fellowship with *God.*
  2. II John focuses on fellowship with the *enemies of truth.*
  3. III John focuses on fellowship with *proclaimers of the truth.*

- John suggested in the book that truth without love produces dictatorial severity, but love without truth leads to blind sentimentality.

- The book can be outlined in the following way:

  1. <u>A word of commendation</u> (verses 1–4).
  2. <u>A word of command</u> (verses 5–6).
  3. <u>A word of caution</u> (verses 7–11).
  4. <u>A word of conclusion</u> (verses 12–13).

INTRODUCTION TO III JOHN
Fellowship Encouraged

- III John offers a stark contrast among three men who respond in different ways to the itinerant teachers sent out by the apostle: Gaius generously gave to others, Demetrius loved the truth, and Diotrephes looked out for himself.

- III John is a personal letter written by the Apostle John to a man in the church named Gaius.

- It is not known for sure where Gaius lived, but it is thought that he belonged to a church somewhere in an area that is now known as western Turkey.

- In those days, traveling Christian preachers and teachers would turn to the local church for hospitality.

- The problem was that some of the people seeking room and board were phonies who just pretended to be true prophets to get free hospitality.

- John was appealing to Gaius for hospitality for Demetrius (v. 12) who was evidently a traveling preacher.

- It appears that the church was dominated by a man named Diotrephes who did not extend a welcome to traveling brethren. In fact, he even sought to excommunicate from the church those who offered such men their hospitality.

- Fellowship is the theme of I, II, and III John:

1. Fellowship with God needed—I John.
2. Fellowship forbidden with false teachers—II John.
3. Fellowship with Christian brothers encouraged—III John.

- This letter gives us a glimpse into the kind of frank and personal correspondence that the Apostle John had with other great Christian leaders.

- This book should cause us to reflect on Christ's values in our relationship with others and the opening of our lives and homes to touching others with His love.

- An outline for III John:

  1. <u>Commendation of Gaius</u> (hospitality, servanthood) (verses 1–8).
  2. <u>Condemnation of Diotrephes</u> (haughtiness, selfishness) (verses 9–14).

INTRODUCTION TO JUDE
Apostasy Unmasked

- The author was Jude, the half brother of Jesus. Mary was their mother and Joseph was the father of Jude. Although Mary was Jesus' true mother, God was Jesus' true father.

- Little is known about Jude. He was one of four brothers (Mark 6:3) and was probably not a follower of Jesus during the years of his brother's ministry. It was only after the Resurrection that Jude became a believer (Acts 1:14).

- The readers are not identified, but we know that they were confronted constantly by false teachers who were immoral, covetous, proud, and divisive.

- Jude warned Christians of these false teachers and urged his readers to "contend for the faith." His purpose was to remind the church of the need for constant vigilance, to keep strong in the faith, and to defend it against heresy.

- This letter is intensely concerned with the threat of heretical teachers in the church and the believer's proper response to that threat.

- Many of the New Testament epistles confront the problem of false teachers, and almost all of them allude to it. Jude went beyond all the other epistles in his relentless and passionate denunciation of the apostate teachers who have "crept in unawares" (v. 4).

- Jude wrote to motivate Christians everywhere with a

three-fold motive:

1. To recognize the dangers of false teaching.
2. To protect themselves against such teaching.
3. To win back those who had already been deceived.

- The false teachers referred to in this letter were probably Gnostics (Colossians 2:4). Basically they said that Christians could do as they please, without fear of God's punishment. This allowed for immoral living.

- While few teach this heresy openly in the church today, many in the church act as though this were true. This letter contains a warning against living a nominal Christian life.

- The book can be outlined as follows:

1. Introduction (verses 1–4).
2. Warnings concerning apostasy (verses 5–16).
3. Guidelines for avoiding apostasy (verses 17–23).
4. Victory over apostasy (verses 24–25).

INTRODUCTION TO REVELATION
The Future Unveiled

* Written by John the Apostle to seven local churches in Asia that represent the entire church body universal.

* Historical records tells us that John was banished to the Isle of Patmos during the time of Domitian. At the death of Domitian, John was liberated and returned to Ephesus.

* Patmos is a small rocky island (ten miles long and five miles wide) in the Mediterranean Sea, about thirty-five miles southwest of Ephesus.

* The theme of the book is Jesus' second coming. According to historians, the approximate date of the writing of this book is A.D. 95.

* The purpose of the book is to reveal events that will take place immediately before, during, and following the second coming of Christ.

* This book tells of the happenings of the last days:

  1. It tells of one last gathering of the Gentiles against Jerusalem and one last battle in which they are destroyed.
  2. It speaks of the last days when the Jews who have been scattered throughout the world will be gathered in the Holy City again.
  3. It will be a time of judgment when God will come like a refiner's fire, and no one will be able to escape the day of His coming.

4. It is a time of terror when mighty men will cry bitterly, and the inhabitants of the land will seek someplace to hide and find none.
5. It will be a time when the universe as men know it will be disintegrated, the stars will be extinguished, the sun will be turned into darkness, and the moon will be turned into blood.
6. It will be a time when those who sleep in the dust of the earth will awake, some to everlasting life and others to everlasting punishment in hell.

- A general outline of the book:

1. Messages to the seven churches (chapters 1–3).
2. Opening the book with seven seals (chapters 4–9).
3. The hour of reckoning (chapters 10–13).
4. God pours out His wrath (chapters 14–16).
5. The defeat of evil (chapters 17–20).
6. God's new creation (chapters 21–22).

ABOUT THE AUTHOR

L ou Nicholes grew up on a small farm in southeastern Ohio where his parents taught him the practical things in life. In July 1954, while on a troop ship headed for Germany, a navy chaplain led him to trust Jesus Christ as his personal Savior. Twenty-six hundred men were on board the ship, and ten came to the meeting, but Lou was the only one who responded to receive Christ.

It was at Philadelphia College of Bible that Lou and I met. We were married at my parents' camp chapel in southern Illinois. At the end of Lou's senior year in college, Paul Bubar, from Word of Life Fellowship, came to speak at a chapel service. He told us he had been asked by Jack Wyrtzen to start a Bible club ministry for local churches. He was recruiting missionaries to go to different parts of the country. Lou knew this was his answer to prayer. He applied and was accepted to pioneer the new Bible club program in the midwestern United States.

It was a great experience for Lou to have a part in developing materials and programs for Bible clubs in local churches. This included Bible studies, quiet-time diaries, Scripture memory packs, followup materials, leadership training programs, etc. In addition to pioneering several types of evangelistic outreaches and starting a camp and Bible school scholarship program for those who wanted to excel in their spiritual growth, he also helped start a program called Teens Involved, which helps young people discover and develop their talents and abilities for the Lord.

God miraculously blessed with 262 Bible clubs in local churches and approximately 1,200 laymen leading them. After twenty-six years, Lou turned this ministry over to other missionaries. He left the Midwest to pioneer a short-term missions program for Word of Life called Youth Reachout. For twelve years, Lou trained and took over two thousand young people to forty-two countries around the world. The Lord worked through the lives of these young people as they ministered in churches, public schools, prisons, hospitals, orphanages, army bases, and many other types of evangelistic outreaches, including open-air evangelism. It was exciting and a privilege to see over forty thousand people of all ages make public decisions for Jesus Christ.

For the past few years, Lou and I have been given another door of opportunity to pioneer. We are representatives for Word of Life in Asia and the South Pacific, where over sixty percent of the world's population is located in Asia alone. A high percentage of these are young people. We have had the opportunity to make various trips into this part of the world. The Lord is giving us unusual open doors to minister, make contacts, recruit potential staff, and help folks come for training, so they can then go back to their countries to reach their people with the Gospel of Christ. We believe God is doing great and mighty things, and we are on the verge of one of the greatest adventures of our lives for His glory. God is so good!!!

With a grateful heart,
Thelma (Lou's Wife)

For More Information

If you would like to receive more information about other books and ministry resources produced by Lou Nicholes, you can reach him by e-mail at lounicholes1@att.net or order books on the Internet at www.XulonPress.com.

CPSIA information can be obtained at www.ICGtesting.com
Printed in the USA
BVOW080355190912

300793BV00001B/16/A